# Teach Kindness First

Library and Archives Canada Cataloguing in Publication

 Murray, Kathleen S., 1977-, author
      Teach kindness first : one conversation at a time / by
Kathleen Murray.

Includes bibliographical references.
Issued in print and electronic formats.
ISBN 978-0-9958085-0-8 (paperback). --ISBN 978-0-9958085-1-5
(PDF)

     1. Kindness.  2. Empathy.  3. Parenting.  I. Title.

BJ1533.K5M87 2016      177'.7      C2016-907158-8
                                   C2016-907159-6

Book layout and design by The Review,
Vankleek Hill, Ontario.
Front cover photo: stokpic.com
Back cover photo: Kim Murray.

Printed by lulu.com
November 2016

# Teach Kindness First

Teaching empathy:
One conversation at a time

**Kathleen Murray**

# Table of Contents

# Foreword

WHEN I was fourteen, my parents bought a cottage and we spent summers there for the next eight years. Needless to say, as a teenager, I was not too keen to be leaving my friends in the city to spend weekends in Vermont. I met Kathleen on my first visit. She came right up to me with a radiant smile and introduced herself. She then quickly ran off to her part-time job at the nearby bed and breakfast. It was a time when the reigning parenting philosophy was *children must be seen and not heard* and discipline was a key value of the Murray household. Her parents were very strict and Kathleen had to earn her keep. Whereas I was moaning about having to go to the country to relax, she had to work. She often accompanied families on their vacations as a mother's helper and she did so gladly. I remember her telling me that working part-time was a small task in exchange for enjoying such a wonderful summer vacation. She always chose positivity, even then. This was the first of many aha! moments I would have, thanks to Kathleen, over the course of our 25-year friendship.

Kathleen's father died suddenly the following summer by the lake at our camp. It was absolutely heartbreaking. Six months thereafter, her mother was diagnosed with multiple sclerosis and she passed away five years later. I remember talking to her on the phone while her mom was bedridden and had lost the ability to speak coherently. Kathleen was studying for University finals. She said to me: 'Why would I feel sorry for myself? My mom is the one who is suffering. It kills me to think that she is in pain and she can't let anyone know, that I can't help.' At twenty years of age, Kathleen, who had been central in raising her then fourteen-year-old sister, accepted that her sister go live with their uncle, an hour's drive away, so that she could continue working and studying to become a teacher. One would think such hardships would take their toll on someone, but not Kathleen. If anything, they have made her a more empathetic person, taught her to express gratitude at every opportunity, and to steadfastly follow her dreams.

That dream today is to give back by helping the next generation hone their communication skills through empathy; a lesson that is more relevant now than ever before. We spend more time scrolling through information and texting than talking in person. According to popular communication studies by Albert Mehrabian[1], tone of voice and body language communicate over 90% of our feelings and attitudes whereas words only transmit 7%. Technology has given us new communication tools but are we saying more...or less? More importantly, do we truly understand each other?

Children are the product of the society within which they are raised; therefore, the onus is on us to show the way. When I became a step-mother, I drew on my own upbringing. I loved story time and the talks my mom and I would have before bed. I implemented those right away with my stepsons. Growing up, dinnertime was for watching the news and we had to remain silent throughout. My brother and I would act out and inevitably get in trouble. The first family rule I created was that cell phones and television had no place in the dining room. Dinner would be for sharing and for connecting. It was a challenge from the beginning as the lure of a text message was strong and the conversation tended to be negative. It actually became much like watching the news: we were covering the day's drama. So, I decided it was time to change our script

---

[1] Mehrabian, A. (1981). Silent messages: Implicit communication of emotions and attitudes. Belmont, CA: Wadsworth.

and start conversations by asking everyone to share the best part of their day. It did not take long for the whole family to come to dinner smiling, ready with fun and positive anecdotes. It is a lesson I hope the boys draw on with their own families in the future.

The time we invest teaching children kindness is time well spent. Once, I fell and twisted my ankle while I was at home with my eldest stepson. I was in pain and I could tell he was very worried. He helped me into the house and to the couch. He then went to get a book and read it to me. He said it always helped him feel better when I read to him. It was the first time I had witnessed him showing empathy. After the story he asked: Stacey, what is the best part of your day so far? He had remembered our dinnertime question and he applied it perfectly, thereby helping to change my perspective. That exact moment was the best part of my day; and my telling him that, was the best part of his. The smallest acts of kindness are often the ones that mean the most.

Before she became an author, beloved teacher, wife and mother, Kathleen was a kind-hearted young girl who made a friend, who smiled in the face of adversity, and who always put others first; whether it be her family or the guests at the Inn. Her positive outlook on life has had a profound impact on me since the day we met. I like to imagine a world where everyone has such a friend. I like to imagine a world where everyone is such a friend. I know we can create it, together, by teaching kindness first.

Stacey Masson
Communications professional,
lifelong friend, and kindness enthusiast.
*Montreal, October 22, 2016*

# Acknowledgments

I am a huge believer that there is no such thing as coincidence. I believe The Universe speaks to us; it's up to us to pay attention. Every time I lose faith along the way, The Universe conspires to send me a sign. In moments of self-doubt, when I asked myself, "Who am I to be writing this book?", messages would come to me from out of the blue from both friends *and* strangers. The timing and content of each message was consistently in line with whatever insecurity I was living in that moment. Thank you, Universe. I am forever in a state of wonder and gratitude.

One might think that by thanking The Universe I would have all of my bases covered, but there are some individual "thank-yous" that must be given.

This book came to fruition thanks to the countless people who have motivated me, encouraged me, taught me, inspired me, and advised me over the years. For every single time that a conversation with a friend, colleague, parent, family member or acquaintance ended with the comment, "Put it in your book, Kathleen!" – I thank you.

To all of the students and the parents with whom I have worked over the years – this book could not exist without our shared experiences. To everyone who has come to me with their stories, seeking advice, thank you for the opportunities you gave me to hone my skills.

To Laura Massé – Nobody said, "It's going in the book!" more often than you. You helped build up my confidence as I prepared for my sabbatical more than you'll ever know.

To Dan Bingham – Our "not so random" phone conversation in September 2014 set the stage for making sure this book would see its day. I remember saying, "I'll just start to write my book, but if it doesn't take shape or I don't like it, I simply won't publish it. It's no big deal." I was really comfortable with this perspective at the time. But you completely refused to accept that from me and shook me out of my comfort zone.

"You will never be completely satisfied with the final product," you said. "You must finish it and you must publish it. There is no other option." Seeing as this advice came from an award-winning comedy writer, I took it to heart.

To Steacy Petersen – No one has witnessed my growth as a teacher and a mother quite like you. Thank you for lending me your ears, your eyes and your unique perspectives. You have kept me grounded and taught me how to go with the flow.

An immeasurable thank you goes out to the Ladies of "Mardredi". This group of fabulous women appeared in my life at the most perfect of times. You witnessed, encouraged, and insisted on the creation of this book in a profound way and you pretty much all appear in the list that follows!

As promised, my La Ruche Crowd-funding contributors get special acknowledgment: Najma Ali, Tanya Angelo, Luca Arnaldi, Marie-Pier S. Beaulieu, Diane Blanchard, Trudy Bosch, Milena Brunetta, Stewart Burrows, Jennifer Campbell, Sandra Chechik, Denise Chevalier, Linda Civico, Dora Colozza, Jason Conyers, Laura D'Adamo, Noémie Desrochers, Kit Dalaroy, Michele Donovan, Lysianne Dupont, Ingrid Enriquez-Donissaint, David Estok, Carol Lynn Frazer, Rachelle Friedrick, Amélie Gilbert, Lorelei Girouard, Sandra Grant, Shelley Hennessey, Manon Henri, France Henry, Julie Houle, Lesley Hutcheson, Nikki Irwin, Barbara Jones, Joanie Lacroix, Sabrina Lang-Moreau, Mathieu Lavallée, Marita Jane Laxa, Émilie Lepage, Karen Macdonald, Laura Massé, Catherine Masson, Stacey Masson, Luisa Mehailia, Jennifer Mellor, Stephen Mellor, Kim Murray, Pam Petrilli, Teresa Picarazzi, Kristen Riley, Stéphanie Paquette, Steacy Petersen, Julie-Catherine Racine, Sophie Reis, Maude Rhéaume, Andria Rieger, La Ruche, Anne-Sophie Schlader, Natacha Silber, Isabelle Sylvain, My My Trinh, Kim Tyrrell, Kim Villarroel, Evie Vourtzoumis, Guy Walker, Jennifer Walker, Devon Warnock-Favreau, Kelly Wood. Thank you so much for believing in me and for investing in this project.

To my text editor, Coralie Clément – you grasped the vision of this project from the very start. Thank you for your keen eye and for your unwavering ability to maintain the focus of this book. There are no words to fully express how much your guidance and expertise kept me going.

To my layout editor and cover designer, Louise Sproule – the final touches you brought to this project are appreciated beyond measure.

To my sister, Kim Murray, for her ongoing guidance in helping me find my place in the world of social media and for being one of my biggest cheerleaders.

To my beautiful daughters, Yasmine and Mikella – you inspire me to be a better me, everyday. Not only have you gladly allowed me to share our personal family stories, but you have also been kind, caring, and patient while I worked. I love you both in a way which words could never fully articulate.

To my loving husband – you have been behind me every step of the way. Your consistent support and your endless encouragement are pillars upon which this project has grown. I love you.

And finally, a heartfelt thank you to my readers. Thank you for joining me on this journey. I look forward to hearing from you, one empathetic conversation at a time.

⌘

# Introduction

Dear Reader,

Here you are holding my book in your hand. I'm hoping that the words "Teach" and "Kindness" caught your attention because they speak to you. Perhaps you are hoping that someone has finally found a way to bring basic human kindness back into our daily lives. With this book, I intend to do just that.

"Who is this book written for?" you wonder. Everyone. If you are a human being who interacts with other human beings, then this is a book you should be reading. My vision is simple: I wish to build a kinder world, one empathetic conversation at a time.

While absolutely anybody can and will benefit from reading this book, you will notice that each script and conversation involves two or more of the following roles: parent, teacher, and/or child. Some of you may already be familiar with my work either from reading posts on my blog or from watching my mini-videos entitled *Gem of the Day*. This book takes all of that advice and elaborates on how to integrate this way of communicating into your own life.

Here are a few axioms upon which this book is built:
- There is a knowingness that something is missing from our society.
- Everything happens for a reason. Life is constantly challenging us, and it is our obligation to accept the situation and embrace the lesson.
- Happiness is not an accident. It is a choice. My ultimate goal is to write a book that will not just inspire but will also teach how to choose happiness.

I am completely convinced that once we learn to speak to one another from a place of kindness and empathy, we will create harmonious relationships that lead to better learning and living conditions. This book will enrich our lives as we learn to understand and share one another's reality.

You will notice throughout this book that I change hats often. At times I speak to you as a mother raising two girls of my own. At other times I speak to you as a teacher with fifteen years of experience. Sometimes I speak to you as both within the very same chapter. This is done on purpose. The book is designed to keep you from choosing to read just the "parenting section" or just the "teacher section". In fact, bookstores are going to be challenged to choose the appropriate shelf for my book because its subject matter encompasses education, parenting, family and relationships, health and well-being, philosophy and spirituality. This book needs to reach teachers and parents especially, but it also needs to reach daycare workers, school administrators, grandmas and grandpas, aunties and uncles, camp counsellors and babysitters. As my editor kindly suggested, "Never mind finding the appropriate shelf. This book needs to be in the front window." If we are ever to live in a kind and empathetic society, it's time we read the same book. Our homes and our schools are at the heart of our communities. Logically, by speaking to the people who occupy these two environments, I ought to cover the scope of society.

Please, resist the temptation to skip ahead to the chapters that address only the issues that concern you. Of course, if you have a burning question that needs answering, go ahead, but be sure to come back to the beginning and read it cover to cover. At the heart of my philosophy is the idea of prevention. This book especially teaches you how to avoid problems rather than waiting for them to appear. I will teach you how to put out unruly fires but I will also teach you how to kindle a fire fueled with kindness and love. Those are the kinds of fires we wish to feed. The kind to which people gravitate. The type of warmth we all ache to gather around, reveling in each other's stories of hopes and dreams.

The scripts I have compiled in this book bring you on a journey into my thinking process. Theory is fine and dandy, but what I find people need most is the concrete, step-by-step "how-to" guide. I am not suggesting that any of these conversations could ever be duplicated word for word, nor should they be. There is no such thing as a one-size-fits-all approach. Human interactions are far too complex for that to occur. Having said that, I sincerely believe that by reading and rereading these scripts many times over, this alternative way of approaching everyday problems will become more natural to the point where you will begin to see a reduction in conflicts, both in your personal and professional life.

It is my deepest wish that parents and teachers alike will read this book and share their realizations with one another. The goal is to foster understanding and build bridges. These conversations have been created based on a multitude of experiences that I have either lived personally or witnessed. Every story is true. I am only speaking about what I know to be possible. If I have not lived it, I will not offer an opinion about it. That's part of withholding judgment, something I insist upon if you're to truly be an empathetic communicator. All of the names in the book have been changed, except for my daughters, Yasmine and Mikella. As for my students and their parents, my friends and my colleagues, everyone's identity has been protected and none of the stories are a complete retelling of a single situation. I fudged grade levels and dates a little, too, just so no one can over-analyze a conversation and convince themselves that I am sharing their particular story.

I hope that this compilation will enable you to develop a deeper understanding of the importance and necessity of integrating empathy into your daily practice, thereby assisting you to address issues in a more proactive and loving manner as they arise in your own life. The only person we can control is ourselves, therefore these scripts are meant to give you a sense of how to guide a conversation by remaining connected to the moment, and reminding yourself to come from a place of love. We need to stop being afraid. When our actions come from fear, we get sucked into old habits and misconceptions.

I have provided you with a list of references and suggested reading at the end of the book. That being said, I will not weigh this book down by citing references and making footnotes along the way. Any claims that I make are based on common knowledge. If you wish to question any assertion that I make, the Internet is a click away. You will surely be able to find any number of articles that can either support or deny what I am saying. Ultimately, you will take from this book that which resonates most greatly with you. I am simply speaking my truth based on my experiences. It is up to you to find your own truth. Take some and leave the rest but know that I mean well in all that I say.

As you begin to integrate this new way of viewing and communicating about important issues in your life, I invite you to share your experiences with me on my blog at teachkindnessfirst.com. Moreover, if you have found this book helpful, please help spread the word by sharing your copy with someone you know or by getting them their own copy if yours is already highlighted and dog-eared. The principal of your school is a great person to start with, since she is in a position to inspire major change in a school climate. The more people we get on board with this fresh perspective on how to communicate effectively by being authentically kind and empathetic towards one another, the more joyful our homes and schools will be and, inevitably, the children of today will thrive in ways we can only begin to imagine.

Please note that you will occasionally hear me speak of spirituality and our soul's journey. You are free to define these terms in whichever way you are comfortable and substitute my spiritual language for whatever terms resonate most with you. An integral part of empathy and kindness for all lies in the need to respect individual religious and spiritual beliefs.

The bottom line is this: when faced with a problem, breathe. Slow down and pay attention to the shift in your energy. Remind yourself that you have the ability to imagine a positive outcome and start creating it with the power of your heart, your love, and your words.

*You must be the change you wish to see in the world.*

- Mahatma Gandhi

⌘

# Part One

## Philosophy of *Teach Kindness First*

Let's explore the meaning and purpose of *Teach Kindness First*. I will introduce you to its four core principles: empathy, motivation, responsibility, and positive desired outcomes.

Part One

# 1

# It's Time We Get Back to Behaving Like a Village

DO you believe it takes a village to raise a child? Your answer to this one question could very well determine whether or not you are ready to embrace the philosophy of this book. While I believe our society once embraced this philosophy, we seem to have drifted away from this way of existing with one another. Before we look specifically at home and school environments, let's take a moment to consider our behavior in public spaces such as grocery stores, parking lots and shopping centers. How many times do children witness adults stealing a parking spot, cursing at the car who supposedly just cut them off, or complaining in line at the checkout counter because the cashier is too slow? Are we showing kids how to be kind in our daily interactions? We can't fault them when they are simply imitating what they see.

I am reminded of ABC's television program series *What Would You Do?* where host John Quinones interviews people who have unknowingly been caught on hidden-camera. The goal of the show is to gauge people's reactions to ethical situations with the underlying question being, would *you* do the right thing in an uncomfortable situation? The show was intended to air for just a few episodes, but it was so popular that it became a full-blown series. I would argue that the appeal of the show lies in the human desire to witness people doing the right thing. The beauty of people standing up for what is right makes this program a regular tear-jerker for me. As a side note, you should know that the tiniest act of kindness can move me to tears. It used to be embarrassing for me, now it's just embarrassing for my daughters!

Back to the show. If it were common for people to always stand up for what's right, do you think the show would have garnered as much attention? Probably not. The wow factor lies in the fact that, as a society, the majority of us seem to be uncomfortable speaking up when it matters most. Sadly, however, there seems to be no shortage of people who are willing to voice negative opinions. To glance at any comment thread on Facebook of a hot-topic issue is to support the accuracy of this claim. I have no statistics to back this up, by the way... this is just my opinion based on my observations.

## Power of One

Change begins with you. And if you doubt the "power of one", I want you to take a moment to consider the global impact of the following individuals: Martin Luther King Jr., Nelson Mandela, Rosa Parks, Deepak Chopra, Oprah Winfrey, Eckhart Tolle... These men and women have had an undeniable impact on the world. Why? They chose to act. They imagined a more beautiful future for humanity and they took actions to be part of its creation. None of them could have fully imagined the glorious outcome of their actions, though they surely dreamed big. Now compare their actions to what I am asking of you. All I want from you is that you join me on this journey towards a society whose members outwardly show compassion and caring for one another. When you see an opportunity to make even the tiniest positive difference in someone's life, I am asking that you give voice to your inner thoughts. Once you get the first words out, the rest will flow. Your first few attempts may not be as graceful as you'd like, but like everything else in life, it just takes practice. You'll be off and rolling before you know it.

Let's examine the following circumstance. Imagine you are in a grocery store when a child starts pitching a fit. What goes through your mind? Do you feel sorry for him or do you pass judgment on him? Although I've never outwardly passed judgment on a parent, I know in the past I have been guilty of being impatient in situations like this. Thoughts such as, "Children aren't being taught how to behave these days!" or, "What was that mother thinking bringing her child to the store when he's clearly exhausted!" would go through my head. Have you ever noticed how much easier it is to judge others than it is to empathize? To put ourselves in another's shoes takes time and effort. It means you have to hold back from jumping to conclusions and actually think about what that person might be going through. Add to that the fact that judging others can make us feel better about ourselves and it's no wonder that we are amazed when we see people doing the right thing, even if they think nobody is watching.

The truth, I have come to realize, is that many parents sometimes feel overwhelmed and at a loss as to how to react to their children and many of them are too proud to admit it. There is so much pressure in today's society to be the perfect parent and very little space for allowing ourselves to ask for help when we need it. It all boils down to pride and it is getting in the way of living a more loving life. It is not for nothing that pride is often considered the worst of the seven deadly sins. It is our pride that leads us to judge ourselves as better than others. While drawing conclusions about what we would or wouldn't do in any given situation can serve us, we rarely judge others with the intent to learn from the situation ourselves. The act of being judgmental serves to feed our Ego. Rare are the occasions where being judgmental serves the one being judged. We have all heard the expression, "Don't kick me when I'm down," and yet that is exactly what we do when we judge a stranger.

Now let's imagine the same scenario with a twist. As you witness a child having a meltdown in the grocery store, the mother turns to you and says, "Any suggestions? I have no idea what to do!"

I can't help but think that you would be less harsh in your judgment. By appealing to you for help, she has openly admitted that she does not have all the answers to parenting. Well, how about that! This is what, "it takes a village to raise a child" can look like. Here is someone who is willing to put herself out there. How often have we actually witnessed this kind of behavior though? Unfortunately we don't see it very often, but the more people who get on board by openly admitting to being imperfect, the more often these instances may occur.

## The Village Mentality in Action

Are you wondering what a fully developed village mentality might look like? Let's take this same grocery store scenario. It is worth mentioning that the following is a true story.

It was four o'clock on a late weekday afternoon when I ran into the store to grab something for supper. As I rushed through the store, anxious to get what I needed, a little girl, no older than four, launched into a fit. "I want Daddy!" she began screaming repeatedly at the top of her lungs. The mother spoke quietly with her daughter, asking her to stop, telling her they were almost done. This did nothing to discourage her daughter's rant. "I want Daddy! I want Daddy!" she continued, tears now streaming down her face. The mother wasted no time getting the things she needed while dragging her child along with her as gently as possible. I discreetly observed the pair, fascinated by the mother's outward air of calm. At no point did she lash out at her child, and after a few failed attempts to calm her down, she simply let her know in a quiet voice that they were almost done. She amazed me. To this day I wonder what was really going on? Had the dad gone away for business? Had the parents split up? Was the little girl angry at her mom and trying to hurt her by demanding to have her father? Had the little girl missed her nap so she was simply exhausted and completely beyond herself given the time of day? Either way, the mother's resistance to engage in her child's meltdown was something to behold.

It would seem that on that particular afternoon we were an unusual group of people in the grocery store. I say this because it was the first time that I ever witnessed such kindness and generosity of spirit from *all* the people in this mother's vicinity. Not one person displayed impatience towards the child's screaming. Surrounding this mother, an air of compassion blossomed. I watched an older couple exchange a sympathetic look that said, "Oh my...remember those days?" The lady standing behind me in line at the cash register smiled and said to me, "A mother's job is never easy." But best of all, was the cashier who spoke to me saying, "Poor thing, that little girl is really having a tough time, isn't she?" Wow. I was so proud of us, this group of strangers thrown together and yet somehow connected on the same wavelength of empathy and compassion. Never have I seen so many adults gathered in one place without at least one person feeling the need to judge the situation in a negative light. It was beautiful. Why is it so rare?

I cannot even count the number of times that I have witnessed judgmental stares in a shopping mall or a grocery store. It's true that more and more parents seem scared to discipline their children in public, but why is that? I get the sense that we are damned if we do or damned if we don't. We are so busy worrying about what other people will think, that we forget to simply do what feels right. When fear of being judged is our motivator, we are doomed to fail. The next time you find yourself in this situation, I invite you to try something new. For one, resist judging the parent's actions. It is none of your business and you have no idea what they have been through so far that day. If the opportunity presents itself, why not make a simple compassionate comment such as, "We've all had days like this before." And to the stranger who is voicing a complaint you could say, "It's people like you who make it hard for a mom to know what to do! Mind your business!" Just kidding! That may be what you're thinking, but instead of addressing the one doing the judging, how about saying something kind to the parent so that the judger can overhear you, followed by a kind smile aimed at the judger, eye contact and all. If you feel the need to say something, I recommend something to the effect of "A smile can go a long way" or "I'm on a mission to build a kinder world. You're welcome to join me."

## We are Human. Period.

Before we even talk about the relationship between home and school, we need to look at our everyday interactions with strangers. What are we doing to take care of one another? We need to be able to handle these everyday situations with basic kindness and grace. At the end of the day, we are all human. We will all make mistakes and they will not always be in the privacy of our own home. If we cannot find compassion for a mother struggling to get groceries done with a toddler in tow, how can we expect to find empathy for the teacher who loses her patience with her students, or the parent who berates his child in front of his friends. We must learn to be less insecure and less fearful of what others think. Let's allow our hearts to lead in the place of our pride.

The next time you feel the urge to tell someone what to do, ask yourself this, "How do I know my way is the *only* right way?" What if I catch my judgmental thoughts, hold back from reacting negatively to another adult's manner of disciplining, and simply observe. I can put myself in their shoes and imagine circumstances that could lead to a child misbehaving in public. Once I am truly in a place of compassion, I can maybe even come up with a few words of understanding such as, "I know how you feel; hang in there." Even just a gracious smile could make a difference. Aside from the fact that you may be helping a parent move though her own fears and insecurities, you will leave with something money cannot buy . . . you will have shown love to a stranger and your heart will feel fuller.

*To empathize is to civilize. To civilize is to empathize.*

– Jeremy Rifkin

⌘

# 2

# Start as You Mean to Go

FROM the moment a child is birthed into this world, an enormous amount of attention is placed on his material existence. Which is the healthiest baby food? The safest car seat? The most gentle and earth-friendly diapers? The list is endless. All of these are important matters, but do we spend even half as much time and effort in evaluating our parenting and educational values? Shouldn't we re-evaluate our beliefs as regularly as we adopt each new and improved gadget that appears on the market which claims to improve the lives of our children? We need to start as we mean to go, all the while being open and willing to change our approach if what we thought would work does not yield the anticipated results.

You have the power to create relationships that fulfill your dreams. To start as you mean to go requires you to look ahead in order to choose a course of action that will serve to bring about the desired results. What kind of relationships do you wish to have with your children? With your students? With your child's daycare provider? With the parents of your students? With the teacher of your child? Do you want the people who care for your child to feel safe and confident in coming to you with their concerns? Do you want to have open dialogue about important issues?

## Our "Dream" Relationship

Since before my children were born, I have always known what kind of relationship I wanted to have with them. I have always dreamed of a day when my children would be grown and we would speak to one another as equals, as friends. I have this image of us sitting at a cozy table in a trendy cafe, chatting easily with one another about anything and everything. I have been sharing this image with them for as long as I can remember.

"Perhaps we're in the Old Port of Montreal...or maybe we're on Dobson Street in Vancouver...," I'll suggest. Now that they're older, they like to make suggestions of their own and they'll name cities and countries from around the globe. It has become *our* dream.

Why did I choose to tell them about this dream from the time they were little? I believe that in sharing my dream of our beautiful, loving, lifelong relationship, I am setting up the conditions under which it may flourish and become a reality. I tell them that as much as I love being their mother, it isn't easy having to make difficult decisions. It is never my wish to disappoint them. But right now, it is my job to be their parent, not their friend. But one day...one magnificent, glorious day...though I will always be their mother and I will always want to look out for them...they will be adults and we can have a friendship wherein I respect their choices and offer advice *only if it is requested*. You may laugh at this last part, but it's true. I may try coaxing them into asking for my opinion, but that's not the same as simply giving it.

I don't pretend to know that this dream will come true. I am well placed to know that life can throw all kinds of twists and turns at us. What I know for certain, though, is that I stand a much better chance at achieving this dream if I consciously work at it in the present moment. Rare are the dreams that come true just by chance.

## Applications for the Classroom

Teachers, don't be shy to ask parents to describe their dream of who their child will become. Ask, "How do you imagine your child as an adult? Describe some of his qualities. Now tell me, what can we do today to help nurture these qualities and make your dream come true?" These types of questions can be especially helpful when you have a parent who is clearly over-protecting their child and is impeding his development as a learner. Sharing a story such as this one is an empathetic and gentle way to encourage parents to cut the strings. Do not expect complete transformations but hold your ground and make your point if you feel the child needs more room to breathe and grow.

Having a clear image of the relationship we wish to experience with a child can help us to keep our eye on the prize and see the bigger picture. Every problem that arises is temporary but the outcome from it can have lasting effects depending on the chosen course of action. Every decision you make is a choice between building a child up or breaking a child down. Ask yourself, "Will my words help or hurt?" Choose wisely.

## Speak Up While They Are Still Listening

I am not well placed just yet to address all the issues we face with teenaged children. I promised that I would only speak of the things I've learned from experience and I intend to stay true to my word. That said, in order for us to start as we mean to go, we need to have a vision of how we wish our children to be as teenagers. "Dream big," I say. Why shouldn't we imagine our children becoming teens who are polite, kind, and respectful, contributing members of society?

How many times have we heard someone say, "Just wait until they're teenagers!" What is that supposed to mean? There is a growing body of research which demonstrates that the teenage brain is going through major changes and does not actually resemble the brain of an adult until the early twenties. Think about what that means in terms of the expectations we hold of teens compared to what they are actually capable of offering of themselves. With everything that is being uncovered in brain research, coupled with what we already observe in teenagers, I think it is fair to deduce the following:

*Teenagers will push the limits.* Knowing this, we can see how starting as we mean to go serves everyone. From the time they were very young, we have been discussing the limits that are set in the home and we have been talking about how the choices we make affect the level of responsibility and freedom with which we are entrusted. My husband and I will ask our girls, "Does it make sense to you that the older you get the less respectful and thoughtful you will become? Does it make sense to you that with age your behavior would deteriorate? Shouldn't the opposite be true?" Since they are young and they are open to making sense of their world, they cannot help but agree with what we are teaching them. These investments in their education will certainly bear high dividends in the future. In fact, we have already begun to see the payoff in our pre-teen.

Do I sound naive or disillusioned? Allow me to elaborate. When my daughters will be teenagers I expect that they will be moody and difficult at times, possibly quite often! At times I may not recognize them at all. I am okay with all of that. What I am not okay with is a total lack of empathy and kindness. In light of this fact, I am determined to instill these values and expectations in my children, day in and day out, *while they are still listening to me* in order to lessen the blow when the hormones hit. And the hormones will hit. But I will not be scared off by hormones. I am willing to talk to my girls until I am convinced that I have made a clear and positive impression. That is my responsibility as a parent. If I don't take the time to get through to them, *someone else will.* I am not willing to risk who that someone else may be...

You may catch yourself saying, "Sure this sounds great, but my child will never buy into this. We don't ever talk like this in our family. She's going to look at me like I'm an alien." (By the way, this is an example of empathy - I am empathizing with you in order to get you to see what I am trying to say. In fact, I have been known to say these very words in parent-teacher meetings in order to make parents see that I completely understand where they are coming from.)

Just because the language and philosophy feel foreign to the family right now is no reason not to start. Every expert in any field was once a beginner.

*Life is an echo. What you send out comes back. What you sow, you reap. What you give, you get. What you see in others, exists in you.*

– Zig Ziglar

⌘

# 3

# Change Your Script

I often find myself in conversations that address that oh-so-delicate relationship between home and school. Many of my friends and colleagues tend to begin these conversations with statements such as, "You won't believe this, Kathleen!" or "Can you imagine? What nerve!" My habitual reaction is to listen quietly while trying to hear what the person is truly saying. When I think I have figured out the root of the problem, I'll ask them to confirm my suspicion. Once my suspicion is confirmed, I'll find a story to tell them that can offer a fresh perspective on the issue. My goal is always to 1) defuse the situation, 2) offer a variety of solutions and 3) (most importantly I believe) find strategies to prevent it from reoccurring.

## Stop Reacting, Start Preventing

What if I told you the reason you struggle in your relationships, be it with your child or her teacher, is not completely your fault. What if it turned out that we had just read the script of life wrong and that all we need to do is look at life through a new lens? We must change our focus from one of reaction to one of prevention. By looking at a situation and opening ourselves up to the idea that there must be solutions to the problem that can keep it from recurring, we inevitably set ourselves up for an increase in our daily sense of joy, peace, harmony, balance, or (what some may call) happiness.

## What Does This Have To Do With Changing Our Scripts?

Our habitual ways of dealing with problems, are just that: habits and learned behaviors. Many of our usual responses to conflicts don't work because the programming we have received is inherently broken. We often fail to look below the surface of a situation for a deeper understanding of why the problem occurred in the first place. To behave like a village means when one of us falls out of balance, rather than making that person "pay" for their wrongdoings, we ought to do everything in our power to help them get back to a balanced state of being. It's what "we must give in order to receive" truly looks like.

## Healing by Truly Seeing

Just because we know better does not necessarily mean we do better. Actual change requires us to apply our new knowledge through action. Part of that action is to simply notice our own contradictions. We have patterns of behavior and beliefs about the way things ought to be that are ingrained in all of us. We must become aware of these and change our internal dialogue in order to start changing how we approach various situations.

For instance, when we do not like the behavior a child in our care is exhibiting, like it or not, we need to look at ourselves first. We may find that we are in a calm state and truly available to the child, in which case we can rule ourselves out as being part of the problem and can simply be there to support and guide him. However, if we realize that we're preoccupied with other tasks, or we are feeling exhausted and impatient, then we owe it to the child to become present in the moment and not fault him for protesting the current situation. Does that mean he simply gets away with throwing a fit at Grandma's house, slamming his bedroom door, or refusing to follow instructions? Absolutely not. The course you will choose to rectify the situation, however, will be very different if you are aware of what you may have contributed to the outburst.

Ironically, as I was writing this, my youngest child, Mikella, approached me and wanted me to play with her. I kindly asked her to give me two minutes. Jokingly she conceded two seconds but her message was clear, "I want your attention". She went off to pass the time with her older sister. Within a few minutes, Mikella started pestering her sister and an argument broke out.

Who was at fault here? Should I have gotten upset with them for fighting? Would that have been a fair response? I would argue that this fight started because I was too busy for Mikella. The two minutes I had requested had passed and I had yet to attend to her.

So the first course of action was for me to be true to my word, stop what I was doing, and go to her and tell her that I was ready to play with her. (Often this is all it takes to stop the progression of a pointless argument.) My eldest had nothing to do with what Mikella was feeling – nothing is personal – but she was the one having to deal with *my* failure to keep *my* word.

If my attending to the situation had not been enough, my next step would have been to articulate the actions I had just taken. This means that I would have literally said, in a kind, understanding voice, "Mikella, I promised you my time and I was slow getting to you. That's my fault, I'm sorry. Let's leave your sister out of it, okay?" If you are new to this way of speaking, you may be met with some resistance and you may need to work harder at it. My daughters have come to learn that I have just acknowledged the truth of the moment and that we can move forward from there, leaving the problem in the past. It's over and we are moving on.

By the way, I was not raised this way. Growing up, the mantra was "children ought to be seen and not heard". The adults ruled the house and the children needed to figure out how to shape themselves around their parents if they wanted to stay out of trouble. I often hear adults today romanticizing these times. I wonder if they've forgotten what it was like to be a kid? Personally, some of the lessons that I learned from that philosophy of parenting were:

- My opinion is of lesser importance, especially if the person is an authority figure, i.e. a parent or a teacher
- I need to keep my thoughts and feelings to myself to avoid painful conflict
- Something must be wrong with me because so much of this way of being does not feel right, yet the adults seem to think it is

I am quite confident that I am not the only person who holds these types of beliefs. However, beliefs like these can lead to a variety of behaviors. For me, I am grateful that it prompted me to learn how to voice my thoughts and feelings in considerate, diplomatic ways in order to feel true to myself while trying not to offend anyone. For others, it may be that they choose to keep to themselves and hide their opinions. It can feel like the easier route after all. It comes at a price though. Avoiding a conversation can keep us safe from confrontation, but whatever issue is bothering us lives inside of us until it finally comes out. It's just that if we do not let it out through words, the stress it creates may show itself through bodily symptoms: lack of sleep, sore muscles, headaches, to name a few. Then we scratch our heads and wonder what's wrong with us.

Here's my golden rule about human behavior, whether it's pleasant or unfavorable: everybody has a reason for why they do the things they do... they just don't always know it themselves. This belief is at the back of my mind every time I deal with a difficult situation. I see confrontation as an opportunity to uncover a hidden pain or sadness, either in myself or in the person with whom I am speaking. In everything I do, the main goal is prevention and healing. We may be having an unpleasant moment, but so long as it leads us back to a place of balance and clarity, then it was a necessary challenge worth facing. Confrontations that lead nowhere are nothing more than a waste of everyone's precious time and energy. It's time we learn to care more about maintaining a healthy body, mind and spirit than about winning a fight or an argument. Let's care less about being right and more about being well. This is how we begin to hush our Ego and allow our True Self to flourish.

## When Does the Past Begin?

What you are reading now is already in the past. The moment you move on to the next word, you are already in a new present moment. That's how quickly the past comes upon us. Think about that for a second. Each experience, no matter how brief, is old within a split-second. The clearer we become about this concept, the easier it becomes to solve simplistic daily conflicts as they occur. The simple act of reading this paragraph and forming an opinion about it has already changed who you were just moments ago. Consider the impact this can have on *every* conversation in your life.

The secret to changing our scripts lies in learning to let go. It means being able to say at any given moment:

- "I don't know why I just acted that way. Sorry about that, can we start over?"
- "Oh my goodness, that was really rude of me. I don't know what I was thinking. Let's try that again."
- "I feel like you're really upset about what happened. I'm no longer concerned about figuring out exactly what went wrong, it's already over. I'd really like to focus on finding a strategy that can keep it from happening again."

Those are the phrases I'll use with adults. It's even easier with kids. I'll declare:

- "OOPS! EEEE-RASE!"
- "DE-LEEEETE!"

That's pretty much all kids need to hear to understand that we are letting go of what just happened and switching gears. If you've ever watched young children at play, then you already know that they are experts at letting go of the past. They show us time and time again what it is to be in the present moment. I refer to this way of behaving as being self-aware, conscious, and our True Self. We are all capable of achieving a higher level of kindness and generosity. It is always a choice.

*Owning our story and loving ourselves through that process is the bravest thing that we will ever do.*

– Brené Brown

⌘

# 4

# Core Principles

IN the previous chapter I introduced some of the key strategies that I use in order to "rescript" our responses to common situations and conflicts. In this chapter, I will break the thinking process down into core principles and explain the importance of each one. Needless to say, I recognize that we do not always have the time to put this much energy into resolving a problem and any given conflict is often more complex than meets the eye. Nonetheless, I firmly believe that by recognizing the importance of these core principles, and by reminding ourselves of them as we engage in challenging conversations, we will immediately notice a positive shift in our own energy as well the energy of those with whom we are engaged, ultimately leading to a more positive outcome.

## Four Core Principles

The Golden Rule states we must treat others the way we wish to be treated. We know this to be true, and yet it is often easier said than done. Where does this disconnect come from? When I sat down to write this book, I had to analyze what it is about how I approach situations that is somehow different from the norm. As I read over the scripts I was composing, a theme emerged. I have pinpointed four core principles that come to my aid, time and time again. They are **empathy, motivation, responsibility, and desired outcomes.**

## CORE PRINCIPLE #1: EMPATHY

Consider the following quotation:

**We judge ourselves by our intentions and others by their behaviour.**

- Stephen R. Covey

I believe Stephen R. Covey is alluding to the fact that we tend to hold others to a high standard and call them out on their mistakes. Yet, somehow, when we mess up it doesn't count because we didn't *mean* for that to happen. To empathize with someone is to be willing to accept that a person's reality or state-of-mind is such that her behavior is the best she has to offer at any given moment. Her best may not meet your standards, but you are not her and she is not you. Whatever the situation may be, it too shall pass. All events are temporary. The more serious the situation seems to be, the more reason why empathy will be your best friend as you work to achieve your desired end results. Empathy acknowledges that we are all human and we all make mistakes. Even if the problem you are dealing with is a recurring one, empathy obliges you to find a way to relate to the other person. Applying empathy helps to ensure that the language we use when resolving a conflict comes from a state of compassion and kindness. Most importantly, through empathy we acknowledge what has happened. There is no room for denial.

Some people claim that empathy does not come naturally to them, however recent research based on MRI scans concludes that "All humans are soft wired to experience another's plight as if we are experiencing it ourselves." (Jeremy Rifkin). This means that we are "soft wired for sociability, attachment, affection, (and) companionship. (...)The first drive is to actually belong. It's an empathic drive." This news is extremely encouraging.

The research goes on to show that if we fail to connect with our core nature and it's repressed due to our parenting, educational, governmental, and business practices, then the secondary behaviors of narcissism, materialism, aggression, and violence will emerge. This helps to explain the root of popular societal beliefs such as, "I shouldn't expect my husband to empathize with me! He's a man!" or "Children are just 'me, me, me!' They're selfish by nature."

Knowledge is power. I believe this research on empathy obliges us to raise our game and evolve emotionally. Developing our empathetic selves can improve our communication skills and make our relationships stronger and more meaningful.

## CORE PRINCIPLE #2: MOTIVATION

We need to make sure that we are speaking up for the right reasons. Pay attention to the thoughts in your head. Is this about proving yourself right? If so, why? Who is running the show here? It's important to make sure that your guiding voice is your True Self and not your Ego. Consider what is motivating you to react to the problem. By react, I mean, why are you feeling the way you feel? If you are nervous about intervening, how come? If you are all too eager to voice your opinion, why is that? Before you engage in a discussion of the problem at hand, you will need to be honest with yourself about what is motivating you to get involved in the first place. For example, a parent may ask himself, "Is this truly a situation that requires my attention, or can I allow my child to maneuver his way through this challenge, all the while supporting him at home?" A teacher may ask himself, "Is my concern more for the student or more for myself? Am I just trying to fit my student into a mold or am I sincerely looking for support from the parents on how to better assist their child?" This is why identifying the purpose of the conversation is very helpful.

## CORE PRINCIPLE #3: RESPONSIBILITY

Every time a problem arises, I ask myself what I could have done differently to avoid the situation. While a problem-free life is not a realistic goal, there are actions we can take to prevent problems from occurring in the first place. When we analyze a situation to see the role that we played in it, we set ourselves up for avoiding those types of problems in the future. I truly believe that a problem will keep resurfacing in my life until I am ready and willing to learn the lesson. We have all heard the phrase, "Why does this always happen to me?" It is one thing to ask the question, it is another to intentionally seek out the answer.

When we teach children to identify and take responsibility for the role they've played in any given situation, whether they were the perpetrator, the silent bystander, or even the victim, we help them learn to rise above difficult situations. In every conflict of our lives lies a gem to be discovered, if only we dig deep enough. I call this gem *empowerment*. It could also be called freedom. However, the secret to discovering this gem and claiming it for ourselves begins with owning our own behavior in an honest and objective way. It is free of judgment.

## CORE PRINCIPLE #4: POSITIVE DESIRED OUTCOMES

It is essential that we take the time to identify desirable positive outcomes in a situation. These outcomes, or goals, will help you establish an action plan. The act of taking responsibility for your own behavior paves the way for choosing a new behavior in the future, one that will serve you better and that may help to prevent a similar issue from arising again. This personal action plan is one that you have complete control over. It does not depend on how others act. Most of the time it is a good idea to share your plan with whomever it is you are experiencing a problem. This way you set the stage for a positive outcome when future conflicts present themselves. Hopefully you'll help to inspire the other person to shift her gaze from the past to the future, which is all that ever truly matters anyway.

Nonetheless, not everyone is going to be as motivated as you are to make better choices. By having a plan that relies solely on the choices you make, you can protect yourself from falling back into the same situation again. It allows you to avoid useless confrontations and to save your energy for more positive and productive endeavors. A personal action plan could be as simple as saying to yourself, "I see that this person is determined to look for a fight regardless of what I say or do. I do not want energy vampires in my life. I choose to no longer participate in a negative dialogue with this person. If I see that the conversation is derailing, I will smile and excuse myself from the conversation." Sometimes the mantra "walk away" is the best one to apply. Walking away is not to be confused with defeat. It is triumph over your own Ego. It means you understand that you are the only one who needs to approve of your thoughts and personal beliefs.

It can be difficult to muster a smile in the face of conflict and you may feel hypocritical doing it. Realize that your smile is more for you than for them. You are smiling to yourself. It is a way of congratulating yourself for taking the high road and remaining centered. As an added bonus, a genuine smile releases healthy endorphins in your body. It, therefore, serves to deflect the negative energy being sent your way and, at the same time, subtly communicates that you are not available for a confrontation.

The only person you can ever control is yourself. There is no guarantee that we will achieve these desired outcomes, but there is no harm in trying. When we expect the best of others they often rise to the occasion. If they don't, at least you know you tried your best to inspire positive change. Not everybody is comfortable with facing a problem, even when it is part of their job description. Depending on the severity of the issue, you can always reassess the situation based on the outcome and see if it matters enough to reach out to someone else for support; another parent, a colleague, the school principal, the school board, etc. So long as you keep into account the four core principles I have just described, you will always know your heart is in the right place.

By no means do I wish to impose a solid framework to something as natural and organic as a conversation, but when we are faced with a challenge, having some concrete guide posts to light the way can be very helpful. Moreover, the order in which I have listed them is not necessarily static. We all think differently and ideas often come to us from all angles. Having said that, to facilitate the process, I will respect this order when presenting the step-by-step scripted conversations.

*Kindness in words creates confidence.*
*Kindness in thinking creates profoundness.*
*Kindness in giving creates love.*

– Lao Tzu

⌘

# 5

# To Attack Is To Be a Bully

BEFORE we dive into the scripted conversations, I need to take a moment to share some of my thoughts and beliefs on bullying. Bullying is a real issue and it needs to be addressed; however, there is a common problem with most of the anti-bullying programs currently in place in many of our schools. Their primary focus is the children's behavior. Yes, you read that correctly. Go ahead and reread that sentence if you need to. I do not mean to offend anyone. Anybody taking a stand against violence is certainly on the right track and is to be applauded. I am confident, however, that the reason why little pink bracelets and anti-bullying slogans have yet to solve the problem (or only have moderate success) is because they often fail to take into account some key players: the adults who are implementing these programs. A violence-free school must start with all the adults: parents, teachers, daycare workers, and administrators alike. We must model appropriate behavior by choosing to rise above any given situation, no matter how upsetting. Yes, I mean it. No matter how upsetting. We are in this boat together, like it or not. Our actions are guaranteed to have a ripple effect. Children are the product of the society within which they are raised. Thus the onus is on *us* to choose wisely. Children will face numerous injustices in their lifetime, just as we do. Like it or not, it is part of the human experience. It is, therefore, our responsibility to model for them appropriate ways to respond. Compassion and empathy go a long way to defuse a problem and inspire positive change. The more competent adults become at implementing compassionate and empathetic strategies to solve their problems, the better able our children will become at resolving their issues with kindness.

## The Authoritarian Society Is a Thing of the Past

Conflicts between parents and teachers are all too common, especially these days. Gone are the days of the authoritarian society when parents supported the teacher 100%, no questions asked. As a child, anytime I voiced a criticism of any of my teachers, it was met with a response that sounded something like, "If the teacher felt the need to speak that way to the kids, then she must have had a good reason." It was followed by something to the effect of, "You just worry about yourself. As long as you know you're doing the right thing, you don't need to worry about others." The good that came from their stance outweighed the bad...most of the time. By supporting the teacher and not lending themselves to the conversation, my parents often inspired me to simply let things go and to go with the flow. When, on my grade two final report card, I came home in tears with a "D" in spelling, they held *me* responsible. It felt to me like that mark had come out of the blue, as I didn't realize I was having trouble in spelling. What if the mark was a transcription error? My parents never questioned the teacher on my behalf. They simply told me to focus harder on my spelling to make sure I'd never get a "D" again. End of story. I'm not sure that was the best route to go. My teacher and my parents let me down in that scenario. I should have either been made aware by my teacher that I was struggling or my parents should have taken a moment to contact the school and give the teacher a chance to explain the mark to me (or to fix her transcription mistake). It's thirty years later and that "D" still does not make sense to me, not that it matters. Although now I see how the perceived injustice of the mark has lead me to be attentive in my writing. There is always a silver lining if we look for it.

## We Can Do Better than Okay

Many of us were raised by parents who preached, "Do as I say, not as I do." This can be a very confusing mantra to live by. It defends the adult's right to scream, blame, punish, etc. and often denies the child any right to defend himself. To refuse to comply with an adult's request was paramount to asking to be grounded for the next week. I'm going to go out on a limb by saying that I suspect this potential history of conflict and pain has a lot to do with some of the problems we teachers are facing today in the classroom. Some of today's parents who felt jilted as children by never being heard by *their* parents over issues they felt to be unfair are now using their voices to stand up to injustices faced by their own children. This is not necessarily a bad thing. We all must hold one another accountable for our actions, children and adults alike. Like-wise, teachers who were raised by authoritarian parents and/or taught by authoritarian teachers may be repeating some of the same behaviors. They may figure, "Hey, it worked for me and I turned out okay." Here's the thing. I'm not certain that we really did turn out okay. Personally, I have needed to do a lot of work on myself to get to where I am today. The self-help section in bookstores has not exploded in popularity for no reason. I am suggesting that we can all strive to do better than "okay".

Of course, we can all tell stories of when being rude has worked for us or someone we know. Whether at a restaurant, a store, or over the phone with a telemarketer, being rude, stubborn, persistent, or even aggressive can work to achieve the desired goal. Though these behaviors may work, being a bully to get what you want is hardly setting the example for your child. And make no exception, schools are a breeding ground for conflict. Sadly though, a shocking amount of conflicts involve the adults, not just the kids. I beg of parents, teachers, and administrators to think twice before engaging in a full-blown argument with each other (it needs to go without saying that is never appropriate to argue with a child). Everyone ought to be considering the long-term impact that modelling bully-type behaviors will have on the children. Moreover, it is not because the argument took place behind closed doors and out of sight from the children that it's suddenly okay. There is always a chance that the story of this incident will be retold in the presence of a child. The point of changing our scripts is to improve the quality of our interactions with others, which has a positive effect on everyone, including yourself.

Parents, it is essential that we never lose sight of the fact that our child will be spending an entire school year with the teacher. Actions taken today *will* reflect on your child and stick with them not only for the duration of that school year, but quite possibly for the remainder of her time at that particular school. Remember, if you are feeling upset, it means you love your child, but you want the teacher to care about your child as well. Your actions ought to inspire the teacher to care about what you are saying, not to resent you for attacking her on her lunch hour. Be clear in your intention before you react.

The same goes for teachers. Chances are if you are feeling upset it is because you care. But be careful. It is essential that when you communicate with the parent about your concerns that you make sure you do not accuse them of not caring enough. In order to achieve a desired outcome, the parent needs to feel understood and supported. If the parent feels that he is being judged poorly for his beliefs or actions, he will likely go on the defensive. Once that connection is broken, it can be very difficult, sometimes near impossible, to repair.

I think most of us would agree that the pendulum has swung too far. As a society in general, we have become too quick to react, too quick to judge. Technology has provided parents and teachers alike with a forum that can be very damaging if not used wisely. From whipping off an email in the heat of the moment to defaming teachers through the use of social media, parents, teachers and students alike are voicing their opinions, whether they are truthful or not. It has become much too easy to lash out at someone without giving any thought to the validity of the accusation. Act first, reflect later has become all too common. When we start to see this behavior for what it truly is: cowardly, then we will start to reconnect with our True Selves. Our natural state is one of love. Too many of us have lost touch with it.

## Never Attack the Teacher

Parents, your child's experience at school boils down to one thing: relationships. Schools are built by individuals coming together with the common goal of educating children. Ideally, those employed by the establishment are there by choice. I suggest that our first instinct should be to assume that everyone wants the best for our child. I am not saying to trust blindly. But adults who have chosen to spend day in and day out, six hours a day, with anywhere from 20 to 35 children in one room, deserve some respect and the benefit of the doubt. Your duty is to trust them; all the while watching, listening, and questioning respectfully and with kindness. Let us agree to only deliberately and outrightly call their intentions into question once we have done absolutely everything in our power to build a positive relationship, and to see the good in the individual. In so doing, we give our child the best possible chance at having a positive relationship with their teacher. Remember, our actions, our words, our body-language, all reflect on our child. Do not kid yourself into thinking that you can be abrasive with the teacher and that she will be inspired to adore your child. (She may love your child even more, out of pity, but I don't think it's a risk worth taking.)

Is that to say that when your instincts tell you that something is wrong that you disregard your feeling? Not at all. Nonetheless, you still must not attack the teacher. Your child still has to go to school the next day. I wish I could tell you that there is no way a teacher would be unfair towards a child because of something you said or did. Teachers are human, too, and it is very difficult to not look at a child without remembering how their parents made you feel. While some teachers are motivated to be that much more compassionate towards a child whose parent has been mean to them, others may feel so hurt that they (hopefully unwittingly) neglect the student because of it. By neglect, I am saying that perhaps the teacher will avoid calling on that child to answer questions in class or she may spend less time assisting her one-on-one at her desk. It may be done unintentionally since as humans, in general, we are often not conscious of how we behave. The teacher may unconsciously avoid additional contact with the child as a means of protecting herself from future conflicts with the parent. Less interaction with the child means less opportunity for something to go wrong that could lead to another complaint. And yes, unfortunately, there are a few teachers out there who would be mean to your child purposefully. So the need to tread lightly should be seen as a tool for protecting and serving your child, no matter how upset you feel about a particular situation. I am not condoning any of this negative behavior, I'm just saying it like it is.

I view a difficult teacher as an *opportunity to teach our children who not to become*. Perhaps that sounds harsh, but it is what it is. We cannot always know why one teacher is more likely to scream and get upset at her students than another. We certainly cannot explain in any reasonable way why a few teachers have the habit of belittling their students or being outright mean to them. While it is fair to say that children do not deserve being mistreated like this, in order to address the situation we must begin with what is in our control, and that is our own reaction. Therefore, our responsibility begins with coaching our child on how to react appropriately. We make sure that our child's behavior is not the cause of the teacher's distress. We hold our child responsible for following directions in class and for doing her work.

As a last thought, before we get underway with our scenarios and scripts, I ask the parent readers to consider the following: society seems to hold teachers to a higher standard than the average person. While there is some sense in doing so, it serves us all to imagine our child's teacher standing in our living room the next time we lose patience with our child. It can be a humbling activity. (Please share your story on my blog when this moment happens for you. Being human is something we all need to share more openly in order to realize our need to resist judging each other and embrace forgiveness more regularly.) Likewise, I ask my teacher and administrator readers to remember that parents do not have all the same resources that we do as teachers. For some parents, the first child they have ever needed to discipline is their own. And for those of us who are both teachers and parents, you all know just how different those roles can be. Our own children can challenge us in ways that our students never have and never will. All of these roles are essential in the upbringing of children. Let's make sure our focus is on supporting one another rather than deferring blame. We sometimes seem to forget that none of us are perfect. We are all here to learn from one another. Education is a lifelong journey after all. As is the pursuit of empathy and kindness.

*Be kind whenever possible. It is always possible.*

– Dalai Lama

⌘

# Part Two

## Applying the Core Principles

Now let's look at how we can implement the four core principles. In each scenario, we will take a "behind the scenes" look at the thought process required to respond to challenging situations.

# 6

# Wrongfully Accused

LET'S consider the following scenario. Your son, let's name him Jayden, has come home with a failing grade on an end-of-term exam. Written in bold red ink are the words, "Clearly, you did not study, Jayden!" When Jayden received his test and saw the note, he immediately explained to his teacher that he did study and that he was confused by his mark, to which she responded, "Then I suppose you need to pay better attention in class, don't you?" Up until now, Jayden has respected his teacher, but this incident has left him feeling embarrassed and uncomfortable. He wishes he didn't have to go back to class. As the parent, you want to support Jayden but you are not sure how. On the one hand you want him to be responsible for his mark, but on the other hand, if he has run into a problem and he is too embarrassed to talk to the teacher about it again, what are you supposed to do? Let's look at a detailed thought process which illustrates how to apply the core principles of empathetic problem-solving dialogue.

**Your EMPATHETIC thoughts towards those involved in the situation may be:**

- It being such a low mark, I can see how the teacher assumed Jayden did not study since he usually does quite well.
- She has so many tests to correct, she may have been feeling overwhelmed.

- She's human, too, and she may have felt disappointed in Jayden and jumped to conclusions out of concern rather than as an actual affront (the way I myself have done before).
- Perhaps she was overtired when she reacted the way she did.

**Now let's make sure your MOTIVATION to intervene is clearly in your child's best interest (and not overbearing, intrusive or unnecessary):**

- Seeing as Jayden has already tried to tell her what happened but she wasn't receptive and now he's too embarrassed to try again, it certainly seems reasonable to approach the teacher yourself.
- If we leave things like this, Jayden may have trouble understanding future content in the course. It seems important to his education that he grasp these concepts.
- Jayden's confidence in his teacher has been compromised and that could have a negative effect on how much he'll participate in future lessons.

**Next, let's determine how you can EMPOWER your child:**

- Jayden and I have already spoken at length about how he needs to be careful to not always assume he "gets it" from the first lesson and then slack off.
- Jayden recognizes that he is responsible for his low mark. His goal is to learn from this mistake and acquire better strategies to avoid this from occurring again.

**Having taken RESPONSIBILITY for some aspect of the incident, your child can articulate the ACTION(S) he will take in the future to help PREVENT it from reoccurring:**

- A strategy Jayden has come up with is that each time more complex material is being taught, he is going to participate more in class by articulating his understanding of the material in order to see if he has indeed grasped it.

**You have clear, POSITIVE DESIRED OUTCOMES:**

- I am hoping that Jayden can have an opportunity to learn the material properly so that he does not fall behind in his studies.
- I am hoping the teacher can offer some form of support.
- I want to be sure the teacher realizes just how much Jayden enjoys both learning and being in her class. (It is always a good idea to let a person know that her efforts are appreciated. Kindness breeds kindness.)
- I want her to know that though her reaction hurt him, he merely needs a little reassurance to know that she does not think poorly of him. (We must never underestimate the importance of feeling accepted.)

With all of this in mind, we are ready to request a meeting or a phone call, whichever is more convenient for the teacher. Unless a strong, positive relationship already exists between you and the teacher, I recommend a verbal conversation when dealing with a sensitive issue. It is so easy to misinterpret the tone and meaning of a letter or an email. When speaking with someone, we have the chance to clarify our point before something we say gets misconstrued and blown out of proportion. The key to addressing a problem with a teacher is to make the *desired outcomes* the guide of our interaction.

The following scripts are reminiscent of those "Choose Your Adventure" books some of us enjoyed as children. They were my favorite books to read because the reader could decide between various outcomes. The author would let the reader choose the heroine's next move. "Should Jessica say 'Yes' to Bobby's invitation to the high school dance? If so, jump ahead to page 75. If not, continue reading on the next page." I would read the book over and over again until I had figured out all of the possible combinations and outcomes. It fascinated me to see how one simple choice could change an entire course of events. Real life is not so different from those fictional books. The outcome of most conversations will depend on the route *you* choose since, at the end of the day, the only person you can ever truly control is yourself. That said, let's begin with an ideal outcome.

"Thank you so much for taking the time to speak with me about Jayden's failing mark. I realize your time is precious," you begin.

"No problem," obliges the teacher.

In a kind, even tone, you continue, "It's just that Jayden was really upset about it. He says he tried to tell you that he did study, but that you didn't believe him? Is that how *you remember it*?" Asking her to tell her version of the story without implying you believe your son over her is key. If you can help it, avoid saying, "Is this true?" There is something about those three little words that can put someone on the defensive even if they have no reason to be.

"I didn't realize he was so upset," she replies, "I just assumed he could not have studied very much if he had failed the test and that by calling him out on it, I would push him to study more next time. He's capable of doing better."

"I understand. I agree that he's capable of better, as does he. He's just always looked up to you and now he feels like you don't believe in him anymore." By saying you understand, you validate the teacher's reaction. This does not necessarily mean you agree with her reaction, but by saying those two powerful words, you acknowledge that she is human, too.

It communicates that you trust she was doing her best in the moment. This puts the teacher at ease and paves the way for creating a positive outcome.

"Oh my goodness. Not at all," she replies, "You know, I guess I didn't realize just how sensitive Jayden can be. Please let him know that I think highly of him. I'll clear things up with him tomorrow in class and I'll take some time with him to figure out where it is that he went wrong."

"I am thrilled to hear you say that. He will be, too," you answer, gratefully.

The very best of teachers will naturally go on to say, "Of course, I'm sorry I made a wrong assumption. Thank you for taking the time to clear up this misunderstanding."

To which the very best of parents will reply, "Thank you for taking the time to speak with me and for being so receptive to my concern. I've already assured Jayden that you meant well! Your response will mean so much him."

As a parent you may be reading this and thinking: There is no way *my* child's teacher would react this way! Well, it does happen, so please give it a try. I know many teachers who have mastered the art of being good listeners and who are capable of humbly admitting when they may have been wrong. Beautiful interactions can and do take place when we allow for each other's imperfections. We must stop holding ourselves and each other to impossible standards of perfection and, instead, see each other's humanness. It takes a village after all. When we assume the best about another person, we tend to bring out the best in that person. It's no mystery why some teachers and parents can have very strained relationships, while other teachers can have very comfortable relationships with the very same "difficult" parents. When we expect the best of others, they often rise to the occasion. It's what is known as a self-fulfilling prophecy.

However, here are some other possibilities as to how this conversation could go and how you can respond in order to lead you to your ultimate goal.

"Jayden wants to feel accepted by you," you begin, "Right now he feels hurt by your comment on his test about not having studied enough. He actually studied quite hard and he isn't sure what went wrong on the test."

The teacher is not in a compassionate mood and replies, "He could not have studied hard enough if he failed!"

Keeping your cool and *your* sense of compassion, you say, "I see where you are coming from but that assumes that Jayden has understood all the material. Is it possible that he needs to be retaught some of the concepts in order to comprehend them properly?"

"We have reviewed the concepts in class plenty of times. Jayden is clearly not paying attention," concludes the teacher, clearly not open to accepting any responsibility for her reaction.

Patiently, you continue to explain yourself, "I hear you. Jayden and I had a good talk about this test and I have to say that he thought he understood. Do you have some suggestions, maybe some online resources to suggest, so that he can figure out where he's gone off track?"

Notice how, in your last two replies, you have acknowledged the teacher's statements. You may not like what she is saying, but you do not waste your energy arguing her points. Rather than debate the truth of her statements, you keep your focus on your goal. At this point in the conversation, the teacher ought to be stumped. You are addressing your concern in a kind and compassionate way. You have not given her any reason to continue on the defensive. You are clearly asking for help in a non-confrontational way. The obvious response now ought to be something like this:

"Okay, I will see what I can find for you to help Jayden. I'll send it home with him by the end of the week," the teacher concedes.

It is natural for anybody to take a defensive stance when we feel insecure or under attack. Teachers are so used to being on the receiving end of disgruntled parents (often unjustly so) that it is only fair we give them a chance to realize we are not "one of those parents" looking for a problem.

I'm not living with my head buried under a rock, though, folks. I know that there are still some teachers out there who are bitter or pessimists or no longer in the right field (if they ever were). This teacher may be feeling so overwhelmed by the ever-growing demands of her profession that the thought of finding extra material for Jayden could send her over the edge. She may blurt out something like, "If Jayden had just paid attention in class he would have understood. I don't have any more time to spend on this. We need to move on. If he didn't get it, too bad, that's his problem."

I hate to admit that there are teachers out there who may actually respond this way, however I must insist you resist giving into feelings of outrage. It will not get you anywhere and only serves to prove to the teacher that you are the one being unreasonable. Instead, I encourage you to take this opportunity to be the teacher for a moment. You may very well sow some seeds of reason. At the very least, by being kind and compassionate, you leave a better chance for your son to be treated fairly by the teacher in the future. An outburst is only likely to damage the teacher's thoughts and impressions of Jayden. A parent's actions will have a direct impact on her child. Whether that impact is positive or negative depends on the level of compassion held by the teacher. This is why it is important to remember your desired outcome of wanting your child to be treated kindly and fairly in class. Therefore, set the example. Be sure to continue using a calm, even voice. Be careful not to sound self-righteous as that will likely undermine the message you are trying to convey.

"It saddens me that this is your response," you say compassionately, "My understanding of the purpose of a test is to determine whether or not the student has learned the concepts. Jayden has demonstrated that he has not understood. I have not asked you to change his mark, I have only asked you for tools to fix the problem. We are talking about a student who enjoys both learning and being in your class. I hear you saying that you believe he has not been paying attention. You may be right. I know for myself anyways that when I think I already 'get' something, I tune out. It especially happens to me at staff meetings...thank goodness there is always someone taking notes or else I would miss out on some important information! I imagine we can all relate to that feeling, can't we? (Pause.) He sees that he went wrong...he just doesn't know where. I get the sense that you feel overwhelmed by the magnitude of the material you need to get through for this term. I am asking you to consider the fact that perhaps, as many of us do, you have forgotten to see the forest for the trees. I understand it is easy to lose sight of what matters most when there is so much pressure coming at you from all directions. That is why I have not asked you to take time from your busy schedule to sit with Jayden and help him. Although that would be nice, I do not wish to be a burden to you. I see how difficult your job is, and I would not trade places with you in a million years. All I have asked for is an opportunity, in the form of an outside resource, that you, in your professional opinion, would suggest so that I, as a parent, can support my child's learning and progress. I am sorry if you felt that I was trying to impose something on you or if you misinterpreted my request. I won't take any more of your time, but I do hope you'll reach out to my son to show him that you truly want what's best for him."

At this point, the teacher will surely wake up from the fog she was under, and respond to you in a helpful manner.

If so, congratulations! You did it! In this last effort, do you see how empathy was used to appeal to her? By using yourself as an example, in the comment about tuning out during staff meetings, you showed her that Jayden is no different from the rest of us. Where there is empathy, there is understanding. Where there is understanding, there is the opportunity for resolution. Now go out there and share your story with other parents to inspire positive changes such as your own!

If, in spite of your best efforts, the teacher still blows you off, I congratulate you, nonetheless, for trying. At the very least, you have hopefully planted a seed of doubt in her mind as to her way of doing things. She may never be able to admit it to you, but she may act differently in the future in other similar situations. Now, if you're anything like me, you may become so emotional as to break down in tears in spite of yourself. That's okay. Let it happen. Tears are a language unto themselves and they often manage to communicate that which words cannot. They may ultimately be more convincing than anything I could suggest that you say. When all else fails, crying just may be what it takes to break through the teacher's shell…I am not saying to force tears, though. Whatever you do or say, it must be authentic.

I know that some of you right now are thinking, "How can she say we must be authentic if we are filtering our thoughts and biting our tongues!" You may feel that a pre-meditated conversation is manipulative and, therefore, not authentic. I hear you, but hear me out. The reason you are planning for a positive outcome is because it helps you to filter out your negative (and often egocentric) thoughts and feelings. The reason you plan to choose your words wisely is because you understand that the prevention of future problems is much more important than having a battle of wills over who is right and who is wrong. The reason you set your mind to focus on the future is to keep yourself from dwelling on the past. All of this gets easier with practice, and eventually it becomes your natural way of thinking, I assure you.

By the way, if, sadly, you do make it to the point where the teacher is completely unreceptive, I encourage you at this point to bring your concerns to the director of the school. Writing a letter similar to the one provided in Chapter 8 allows for this interaction to be on record. Once a teacher has tenure, it can be very difficult to move her out of the classroom, even if it is no longer the best place for her. Hopefully, the principal will be able to influence the teacher's perspective and inspire her to be more receptive in the future.

*I am convinced that life is 10% what happens to me*
*and 90% how I react to it.*
*And so it is with you . . .*
*we are in charge of our attitudes.*

– Charles R. Swindoll

⌘

# 7

# Priorities Are Allowed to Vary

WE hear a lot these days about the importance of living a balanced life. However, the definition of a "balanced life" is likely to vary from one person, and one family, to another. We have probably all completed those little quizzes that ask us to place in order of importance what we value most: family, health, work, education, relaxation, and friends. Have you ever heard of an entire room of people placing all six options in the exact same order? Of course not. Everyone has the right to place any one of these six options at the top of their list and to behave accordingly. We will not always agree with the choices other people make. Student absences is sometimes a consequence of this prioritization. Absences can be quite frequent and can create headaches for teachers who already feel overburdened by their ever-increasing workloads. There are so many reasons for which a child may be absent: illness, sporting events, competitions, family obligations...the list goes on. Some of these reasons tend to be perceived as more legitimate than others. One that is often criticized is the family vacation. Personally, I feel that something as pleasurable as a vacation should not become a point of contention between parents and teachers. Parents get to raise their children as they see fit. Having said that, as with anything else, our expectations of one another must be reasonable. Since this is often a touchy subject for many parents and teachers, it seems like a good example for modelling the core principles. What I'm proposing is that we ought to respect each other's choices, discuss the possible outcomes, and come up with a reasonable plan in a polite and considerate way.

Here is an example of the type of email a teacher may receive concerning a student's absence:

Dear Teacher,

Our family will be on vacation for the week of (insert dates). You can send home the work that my child will miss and we will make sure she gets it done.

Thank you,
*Parents*

How should a teacher interpret this letter? Should he feel as though a demand is being placed upon him? Or should he simply be glad that the parents are informing him of their child's absence and requesting work so their child does not fall behind? We get to choose how we respond to situations. What if we were to be kind with each other and take each situation on a case-by-case basis?

**A teacher's EMPATHETIC thoughts toward the family may be:**

- I know how much I enjoy my three months off a year. I can't imagine only having two weeks off a year, as is the reality of many families.
- I realize that it can be challenging for parents to coordinate their (limited) vacation time.
- I know that employers cannot necessarily grant vacation time to every parent in accordance with the school calendar, especially during the Christmas holidays or spring break.

- I understand that some families may only ever be able to afford a vacation if they travel off-season, and that means travelling during the school year. Everyone is entitled to travel if they can find a way.

**A teacher's MOTIVATION in his response may be:**

- I realize that a major part of teaching is building relationships and this is a great opportunity to show understanding and compassion.
- I want the parents to know that I (choose to) respect their choice and that I will do what I can to support their child.

**A teacher's RESPONSIBILITY towards the situation:**

- Though I am not responsible for the decision which has been taken by the parents, I *am* responsible for my attitude towards the situation and my priority should be to take the student's needs into consideration to the best of my ability.
- I can easily assign work that I believe the student can complete with relative independence and success, but I am not obliged to spend an excessive amount of time preparing work for the student.
- I am responsible for setting and respecting my limits.

**A teacher's ACTIONS and DESIRED OUTCOMES:**

- The ultimate goal is for the student to feel supported.
- My reaction sets a tone for the student's vacation. It ought to be kind.

## THE OTHER SIDE OF THE COIN . . .

Here is what I propose for parents.

### The parent's EMPATHETIC thoughts toward the teacher may be:

- I understand that it is my choice to take my child out of school and this choice most likely represents additional work for the teacher. I should only request the work if I sincerely believe my child will have time to complete it. I do not wish to waste anyone's time.
- I understand that I must respect and accept whatever decision is taken by the teacher; professional judgment must be left up to the professional.
- I realize that many lessons are dependent upon in-class instruction and therefore my child will inevitably be missing out on certain activities. It may impact my child's grades to a certain degree, and I must accept that as a natural consequence of my decision.
- I recognize that I will be the one responsible for my child's learning during the family vacation.

### The parent's MOTIVATION to communicate may be:

- In order to be a true team player, I must be honest with the teacher about my child's absences, and that means informing him ahead of time out of common courtesy.
- I want what's best for my child, and while I know that there is no shame in admitting that we have decided to "unplug" for a family vacation, I also realize that the teacher is working hard every day to plan lessons for my child. He deserves to know if my child will be absent for something important.

70

**The parent's RESPONSIBILITY towards the situation:**

- If I prefer to have my child catch up with school work after our holiday, then I must be willing to put in the time and effort.
- I must prepare my child to accept the fact that he may miss some free time or recess periods in order to catch up on important work.
- Ultimately, I must take responsibility for my choice to pull my child from school for a vacation. I must not make the teacher feel pressured or hold the teacher accountable for my personal choice.

**The parents' ACTIONS and DESIRED OUTCOMES:**

- If I do request school work for during the vacation, then I must do my best to ensure that my child completes the work punctually and with integrity.
- It is essential that I show appreciation for any and all efforts that the teacher makes on my child's behalf.
- Everyone should feel good about the plan put in place.

It is just as much the teacher's professional obligation to respect the family's choices, as it is the family's obligation to respect the limitations of the teacher. When everyone chooses to put the child first, the lens shifts to the most important player. We must simply ask ourselves, what is best for this particular child, in this particular situation? The teacher must accept that the student will be gone. To resist that fact is wasted energy. To spend time complaining about it is equally futile. I would never want my vacation to be perceived as a problem for someone else. I would want them to be happy for me. Life is short. When opportunities to enjoy life to its fullest arise, we ought to seize them. Having said all that, some parents do not inform the teacher of their child's absence until after the fact. I wonder if it's because they are worried about the response, so they avoid saying anything. My hope is that this illustration will make everyone feel more confident about discussing any topic, including this one, in a proactive and cooperative manner.

## BUT IT *CAN* BE A PROBLEM. . .

I know, I know. In spite of everything I've just said, sometimes student absences can create problems. Students may miss a major evaluation or an end-of-term exam. Sometimes the teacher is then asked to take his personal time, such as his lunch hours, to help get the student caught up. I think it's time we come up with creative solutions to this ever-growing reality. Ideally, parents would look at the school calendar and contact the teacher before they book their vacation to avoid a conflict with important end-of-term exams. This is especially important if they know their child has upcoming entrance exams to high school or college. Since this is not always possible, the bottom line needs to be that there is zero pressure and zero expectations placed on the teacher due to a student's absence for a personal family decision. To be fair, parents who book their trip in advance to save on costs often do not have access to the exam schedule since it has yet to be determined. Ideally, those responsible for exam schedules (government and school boards alike) would become more sensitive to the reality of parents and provide these schedules much earlier in the school year. Likewise, it's time that parents be ready to take responsibility for the choices they make.

In that vein, I would also like to suggest that principals and school boards support their teachers by putting a policy in place that holds the parents responsible for making sure their children complete mandatory exams that they miss and that this should not be an extra burden to the teacher. For instance, many teachers offer after-school tutoring. A simple, low-cost solution would be for the parent to hire a tutor to monitor the exam. Another possibility would be to offer make-up sessions, perhaps at the school board. The parents would pay a small fee to cover the cost of the supervisor. No matter what, we can surely come to an agreement that works for everyone involved.

Ideally, school-wide policies would be put in place to make these conversations much easier to manage (or to avoid them altogether). There are so many reasons why families vacation during the school year. We may or may not agree with their reasons, but what's the point in judging them for it? Ultimately, the decision is theirs. This is their life, their child. Teachers need to learn to draw the line between what does and does not concern them. When we say that it takes a village, part of that philosophy embraces the notion that we care for each other, first and foremost, and that means respecting each other's dreams, especially when it comes to choosing how to achieve a balanced family life.

*We are always getting ready to live but never living.*

– Ralph Waldo Emerson

⌘

# 8

# The Unhappy Teacher

TEACHERS have a professional obligation to guide their students with honesty and grace. It goes without saying that we all end up connecting with some teachers better than others. That's normal and to be expected. Teachers have their own personalities, styles, and approaches, as do students. No matter how a teacher perceives her students, her professional duties must be unwavering. When a teacher is faced with students who lack motivation, her first instinct ought to be to ask her herself, "Why?" and to make an effort to inspire her students to rise to the challenge. A teacher who is repeatedly unkind and unhelpful towards her students is not fulfilling her obligations. There may be very good reasons for this. She may be burning out. She may need help. We can apply the philosophy of "It Takes a Village" and reach out to offer help. If nobody ever says anything, how can we hope for the situation to ever improve?

I am reminded of an unpleasant experience in my senior year of high school. I had always been strong in math, and I was used to being the person everyone came to for help. Due to some unavoidable absences from class, I had missed several introductory lessons in pre-calculus. For the first time in my educational career, I had fallen behind. I wasn't used to struggling. So my pride took over and I spent the last few months of that school year telling my teacher, Ms. Withering, that it didn't matter anyway, because I had been accepted to a business program. I believed that calculus was for science students and that I did not need to learn this kind of math. Her only response was to look at me and smile. I knew she had taught for years at the college level so I assumed that, if I was wrong, she would have told me and offered to help me get back on track so that I could be successful in my pursuit of a business degree.

I wish I could give her the benefit of the doubt and say she had no idea how incredibly relevant those math lessons would be to me, but time has chipped away at my naivety. Experience is an excellent teacher, and I can see her more clearly in my mind's eye. I see now that she was not a happy person. I see how for her, this was revenge. Earlier in the school year, when students had difficulty understanding a concept she was teaching, I would offer my help by pointing out an implicit step that she was forgetting to explain. I did this respectfully and, since my explanations were met with gratitude from my classmates, I thought that I was being helpful. Her insecurities in her effectiveness as a teacher are surely what fed her choice to not assist me. She must have been thinking to herself, "Ha! Wait until she gets her math syllabus. What a wake-up call that will be! I'll teach her a lesson!" And a wake-up call, it was. My first (and only) math class in the business program was quite the rude awakening. Fortunately, when I explained the situation to my professor, he showed me compassion and offered me support to ensure I passed his class. I transferred to the education program the following semester. I do not regret my decision in the least but I wish I had been better informed. The most significant lesson Ms. Withering taught me was about what *not* to do as a teacher.

## Ask the Right Questions

Knowledge is power and it ought to be every teacher's mantra, without exception. Any adult who intentionally withholds relevant, life-changing information from a child is failing at her job. Teachers are responsible for providing children with as much information as possible so that they can make informed decisions about their future. Moreover, if, as a teacher, you are having trouble being understanding towards your student's behavior, instead of giving up, perhaps you could seek out more information on your student. My absences were due to the fact that I was taking my mother to doctor appointments. She had just been diagnosed with Multiple Sclerosis. At the time, I was her main caretaker since my father had recently passed away. I wonder if she knew that about me? When we lack compassion for our students, we risk failing them in more ways than we can imagine.

Lucky for me, I was a young adult when I had my first experience with an unhappy teacher who caused me harm. Some of us are not so lucky. What should we do as parents if our child comes home complaining about his teacher? Let us play out the scenario of a teacher whom we feel loses her patience too frequently in class and your child is having to deal with this negative energy on a regular basis. Your belief as a parent is that your child is doing what's expected of him. Using the core principles, we will discuss what to teach your child and we will explore what we can do to inspire positive change.

**Your EMPATHETIC thoughts toward the teacher may be:**

- I can imagine it is not easy to get 20-30 students to pay attention and do their work.
- She may not see the harm she is doing because no one has ever voiced a concern.
- Her behavior may seem perfectly acceptable to her. She may be simply using the strategies that were used with her as a child and she sees no harm in such techniques.
- The teacher may be feeling burned out or is dealing with personal issues at home.

**Your MOTIVATION to intervene may be:**

- I want my child to have a positive experience in class.
- I want my child to know that I support him.
- I want the teacher to realize the impact her negativity is having on her students.

**Your RESPONSIBILITY towards the situation:**

- It is my responsibility to teach my child how to be a well-rounded person.
- Although I wish for all the adults present in my child's life to lead by example, I must accept that ultimately I cannot control their behavior.
- I am not comfortable with what my child is telling me about the teacher's behavior, therefore I feel compelled to address the issue.

**Your ACTIONS and DESIRED OUTCOMES:**

- To teach my child that we have the right to expect and request a positive learning environment.
- For my child to see me as a positive role-model by communicating our concerns respectfully.

With all of this in mind, we are now in a good place to speak with our child about his experience with his teacher. In my family, our best conversations take place around the dinner table and at bedtime. Get to know when your child is most open for discussion and choose one of those moments for this chat. Let's name your child Justin. This has been an ongoing problem and tonight, over dinner, you are ready to take actions towards finding a solution.

"So, Justin, how was class today?", you ask in a conversational voice.

"Fine, I guess," Justin replies, adding in a sarcastic tone, "Of course, Miss Roberts spent the afternoon screaming at us for nothing again, but that's nothing new."

"What were you doing while this was going on?" you inquire. You are careful not to imply that he may have been part of the problem, but at the same time, you are not so naive as to think it is impossible for your child to misbehave.

"Don't worry, mom," your son reassures you, "I was quiet and did what she asked of me."

"What were some of the other kids doing?" you ask.

"The usual. Talking to each other when they should be working. Her idea of control is to yell at us, but no one cares enough to listen. We're not learning anything," he says.

Here is an ideal opportunity to show empathy. "We've all had teachers like that, Justin," you explain, "I wish she was less impulsive with her anger. At least she is teaching you what not to do in life when it becomes your turn to lead others."

"Whatever that means..." he says under his breath.

You are careful to be patient with his reaction. He has a right to feel upset and dismissive about the situation. It is your job to teach him how to see things differently. "It means that it's all about attitude," you explain, "So even though it's not fair that Miss Roberts has a short temper, you are in control of how you react to it."

"Yeah, I kinda know what you mean. I don't really get upset when she's yelling 'cause I know it's nothing I did wrong. It's just irritating. It's not how I want to spend my afternoon," Justin replies.

"Every time you find yourself judging her inabilities just remember that one day people will be judging you. If there's nothing else you ever learn from her, let her be your guide as to whom you do not wish to become. There is no need to punish her or give her a hard time for it. That would just reflect poorly on you. Show kindness, tolerance, and compassion. Look for things you enjoy about her class and let her know about it. Try to notice when she is kind and see if you can give her a compliment on it without being too obvious. It may inspire her to change. It's worth a shot anyways." I know this may sound like too much to ask of a child but I don't think it is. He may never actually say or do any of those things, but you have planted some seeds for the future. You are influencing his perspective on life in general.

"That makes me think of how you've told me that how I act says more about who I am than the person I'm talking about," he states.

"I love that you realize that, Justin! You're absolutely right. If you go around acting superior to her or being unkind, the person who will look really bad is you. Carry yourself with grace and you will go far in life," you conclude.

A dialogue such as this one will surely be revisited in the future and the two of you will be able to continue philosophizing on how to turn negative circumstances into opportunities for growth. This conversation has allowed you to successfully honor your child's feelings and you have guided him on his journey towards adulthood.

## Where Do We Go from Here?

In terms of addressing your child's behavior, mission completed. However, you may not be comfortable leaving things like this. The question becomes, "Is it acceptable that the teacher continues in her ways without any attempt on your part to inspire a positive change?"

I encourage you to talk with other parents to see if they share the same concerns. It's important to equip children with the tools necessary to cope with difficult people, but we still want them to be treated with kindness. If we feel the behavior is negligent or abusive, we ought to address our concerns. Here is a letter you could write to Miss Roberts. You can use the same language if you prefer to make a phone call.

Dear Miss Roberts,

Hello. I hope you are well. I was wondering if you could give me a little insight into how Justin is adjusting in class. He often talks about his day and the feeling I am getting is that he is having trouble focussing on his learning. Have you noticed anything? I realize you may need some time to observe him before you get back to me. Feel free to write me or give me a call if you prefer we speak in person.

Thank you for your time,

Sincerely,
*Your name and phone number*

This letter gets the ball rolling. It draws the teacher's attention to the fact that one of her students is having difficulty in her class. She may be surprised to hear this. Once you hear back from her, you will have the chance to express how your son feels it gets too loud in the class. It will be for you to judge whether or not you feel comfortable asking her about her discipline techniques. She may be open to the conversation, and she may confess that she finds herself losing her patience quite often. If so, you proceed compassionately. You are empathetic and you do not pretend to have all the answers. It is more likely that she will defend her methods. If so, I contend that it is not your place to offer suggestions. It is likely to feel too threatening to the teacher to receive this type of feedback from a parent.

Personally, I would find this conversation very challenging to have. I would hope that by telling her that my child is having trouble concentrating in her class, and by encouraging other parents to do the same, that she would realize that her actions, though behind closed doors, are not going unseen. I would never attack her methods, since it's too risky that Justin could become a target of her frustrations. Remember, your goal is to improve the situation. No one mistreats others unless they are struggling.

If after a few weeks, nothing changes, I would contact the principal. Your motivation and focus continue to be for the good of the school. You are never to attack. Otherwise you are no better than the teacher. I suggest a simple letter such as the following.

Dear Principal,

Good day. I would like a moment of your time to share a concern. My child, Justin, has been telling me that Miss Roberts is often screaming at the students and it makes for a difficult learning environment. I have spoken with Miss Roberts concerning Justin's difficulty concentrating in her class. I hoped that by contacting her, she would realize the cause of his stress. I believe teachers ought to model speaking to one another kindly. I understand that we all lose our patience sometimes, but this behavior seems to be the rule rather than the exception. To me, this falls under the category of bullying. It is in light of the school's anti-bullying policy that I feel obliged to communicate these concerns. Justin is aware that I am writing you and he is a bit worried that she will begin to single him out. I assured him that you would be discreet. We bear no hard feelings towards Miss Roberts. Our wish is that the school will be able to offer her support and teach her how to effectively implement alternative discipline techniques that do not attack the children. I hope that you know my heart is in the right place. Your time and attention is greatly appreciated in this matter,

Sincerely,

*Your name and phone number*

Positive outcomes are much easier to achieve when we choose a route of compassion. This does not mean we must accept whatever has happened. It means we accept that we cannot *undo* what has happened, all the while seeking positive change.

*Any fool can criticize, condemn, and complain*
*but it takes character and self control*
*to be understanding and forgiving.*

– Dale Carnegie

⌘

# Part Three

## Let's Just Talk

Now that we've analyzed how to break down the thinking process, we will explore a variety of challenging scenarios wherein the core principles are woven into the conversation organically. Challenge yourself to identify them as you read and take a moment at the end of each chapter to reflect on how you will proceed the next time you find yourself in a similar situation.

# 9

# What if Screaming is All I Know?

I had several potential titles for this chapter, a couple of which were; *Why Are so Many Kids Growing up in Angry Homes? and Stressed out Adults = Stressed out Kids*. This chapter is based on the idea that our classroom ought to feel like an extended family. Though I still hold this belief close to my heart, I have needed to reframe my philosophy in light of certain discoveries.

Each new school year, on the very first day of class, I pitch my philosophy to my students. "Since we will be together nearly six hours a day, five days a week, for ten months, that makes us a family," I begin. "Therefore, I expect us to treat one another as such."

The first year I implemented this philosophy, it took me until March to realize why I was having trouble making it take hold the way I had hoped and imagined. In my mind, reminding the students that we should treat one another as a family ought to have motivated them to be kinder to one another. Anytime I would overhear unkind words or witness mean actions amongst my students, I would say, "We are a family. We should be kind to each other. Try again. Make it right." Many of my students reacted positively to this philosophy by either changing their tone of voice or by demonstrating greater respect towards their peers. However, with certain students, not only did their behavior not improve, but I even sensed a heightened level of agitation.

I finally understood the underlying problem when, one afternoon, seven months into the school year, ten-year-old Fred blurted out, "Miss Kathleen, what if screaming and yelling in a family is all you know?" His words hit me like a ton of bricks. Our eyes locked, and in that moment I saw that he knew he had just taught me an important lesson. The whole class fell silent as Fred continued, "I have never heard my parents work out a problem without screaming at each other...I hate it!" His last words caught in his throat as he choked back his tears. His passionate confession echoed throughout the classroom.

"It's the same thing in my home..." called out one of his peers.

"I feel you, man," offered another.

Suddenly, whatever issue it was that had prompted Fred's outburst no longer seemed to matter. We had delved into a much deeper level of conversation, one that had to be handled delicately and compassionately. It is not for me to judge such a statement. Every family has its own story, its own baggage, its own set of values. *Each family is on its own journey.* Fred's statement may have been completely true, but it was not my place to probe. Was the family under enormous stress? Had someone lost a job? Was the marriage suffering? The answers to any of these questions were none of my business. (Fred would perhaps decide to confide in me, but if so, I would like for it to be on his own initiative. In Chapter 17, I talk about the need for the classroom to be a "safe zone" where children are invited to leave their troubles at the door. While the students know that they can trust and confide in me, I believe I offer them a certain comfort when I offer them their privacy.) Ideally, my response needed to be phrased in such a way that acknowledged his statement as *his truth,* and supported him on his journey, without talking against his parents in any way, since I could not pretend to know or understand the whole situation. I needed to resist making assumptions.

My response to Fred needed to have the utmost respect and empathy possible. If we were to break it down into steps, still mirroring the core principles, the process would look something like this:

## Empathetic Thoughts

I needed to acknowledge his feelings without speaking against his parents. "Fred," I said, "Clearly the arguing you hear in your home is very upsetting to you. I am sorry that this is your reality. For me, growing up, my parents never argued in front of me. I should have realized when I've been saying 'We must treat each other as a family,' that that experience is very different for each of us."

## Motivation to Respond

I needed to recognize that this claim, while true in Fred's eyes, could very well have another dimension to it, of which I was completely unaware. I needed to focus on reassuring Fred that, in our classroom, he should not have to deal with screaming and yelling. That is a professional responsibility I take very seriously. (That is not to say that I never lose my patience or raise my voice. Any parent who has been pushed to the edge by his couple of children can surely comprehend that a group of 20 to 30 students can have a way of pushing anyone to the brink. Having said that, I am careful with my words, even as I lose my patience. No form of verbal abuse is ever acceptable.)

"I don't think I have to tell you how strongly I feel about speaking to one another kindly. I can't change what goes on at home for you, Fred, or any of you for that matter. The point I've been trying to make since August is that there is always a way to solve our problems using kindness and respect. I should have realized that it can be different for each of you at home and that if you have not had this modeled for you, then it would be that much harder for you to know how to fix your problems peacefully."

## Responsibility

This is a delicate situation. While in my heart I wish that children could be spared from certain stressful realities of home life, I must acknowledge that this is out of my control. My responsibility towards my students is restricted to the relationship we create with one another, within the four walls of our classroom. (Unless there is suspicion of an unsafe situation for the child, of course.)

"Boys and girls, can I ask you something? When I've been saying, 'We should feel like a family and treat each other as such', have you understood what I've meant?"

"For sure, Miss Kathleen. We know that it has to do with getting along," offered one student.

"It's just that sometimes I find we get along better in the classroom than I do with my own family at home," said another student.

"We're really glad this is what you teach us, Miss Kathleen!" chimed in a handful of children.

## Action and Desired Outcome

The action I needed to take was abundantly clear. I had to continue insisting on these family values that I hold so dear as the students were clearly showing their appreciation for this approach. However, there was a need for me to reframe it so that I could be more sensitive to the variety of realities my students experienced outside of the classroom.

"I guess for some of you, screaming is just normal in your home," I remarked.

"Oh, yeah!", "You bet!", "No kidding!" several students called out.

"Judging by what you're telling me, though, you would prefer to live with less of that type of behavior and you are glad I insist on speaking to each other kindly in the classroom. There are ways to solve our problems that do not require the use of anger. If ever you find yourself teaching these lessons to your family and inspiring positive change in your home, that would be so wonderful."

"I doubt it, Miss Kathleen," interrupted Fred.

"Fair enough, Fred. That's probably too much responsibility for a ten-year-old, isn't it? Can we at least use our experience in this classroom as proof that it's possible to live peacefully with others and that when conflicts arise, we can often solve them without yelling and without making mean comments? Hopefully this could help you to visualize one day raising your own family in a peaceful environment. You would know that it's *possible* because you will have experienced it. Do you like that idea?"

"That works for me," replied Fred. Several more students spoke up to say they liked that idea as well. While I dare not claim that this conversation was some kind of miracle that changed their behavior for the rest of the year and that no more arguments or confrontations ever broke out again, it was certainly a significant moment for the group. My relationship with Fred, for one, took on a whole new dimension. He clearly felt a sense of relief that someone understood him on a whole new level, and while, naturally, conflicts still arose, it was clear that he desired a positive change in his life.

I no longer take the philosophy of treating one another as a family for granted. These days, when I introduce the idea to my students, we discuss what that could mean and how we want it to look. When the children list less desirable aspects of family life such as yelling, being mean, and saying rude and judgmental comments, I ask them if they want to include these as part of our classroom agreements on how we ought to treat one another. The resounding "No way!" that these ten-year-olds cry out is something to which we all should be paying closer attention.

Nowadays, I still believe that our classroom ought to feel like an extended family, but I emphasize the idea that we must create and/or reinforce the habit of treating each other the way we wish to be treated, anywhere and everywhere we go, because it always feels good to be treated with kindness. I find myself asking my students if they think it is possible to live harmoniously with one another. We talk about what makes it challenging and how we can deal with those challenges. Fred's bravery in speaking his mind and in sharing something so personal created a ripple effect that is ongoing to this day.

*Turn your wounds into wisdom.*

– Oprah Winfrey

⌘

# 10

# Acts of Kindness

AN act of kindness is exactly as its name states. It is any action that is kind. There is a beautiful video created by Life Vest Inside, and available on YouTube, entitled "Kindness Boomerang" which I have been showing my students for years now. The song "One Day" by Matisyahu carries us through a series of events involving interactions among strangers. Each mini-event represents a problem or a struggle and how simple, kind gestures from strangers can help to make things better. Moreover, the ending illustrates that we are all connected and the positive energy we send out into the world can come back to us in an unexpected way. There is always at least one student, upon viewing this video, who will blurt out, "That's karma!" I love that this word is already in the vocabulary of some eight-year-olds. I then give that child the opportunity to explain their understanding of the term to the class and it consistently leads to an enlightening conversation on how we are responsible for the attitude and energy we bring to any situation. In simple terms, I'll tell them, "We get what we give."

It is in this vein that I will teach the kids that one of the most effective ways to break a bad habit is to replace it with a better habit. Rather than making a child feel bad for a negative behavior such as hitting or screaming, I label it as a bad habit. This helps to disassociate the person from the action. This belief system assists me in convincing children who have well-ingrained negative behaviors that they are innately good people. They simply need to practice new reactions that bring more peace and joy to their lives and the lives of others. When a child who is used to being seen as bad is given the chance to show others he can do good, miracles can happen. I have witnessed children who start out as virtual outcasts in the classroom become some of the most popular kids by the end of the school year. That's not to say that these children have completely transformed and no longer run into problems. The magic lies in the fact that the other children in the class have had the chance to see their goodness and can identify with their struggle to make the right choices. Once again, we see how acts of empathy provide us with concrete evidence of how we are all innately good and trying our best.

In adult terms, how many of us have a friend who has, let's say, quit smoking, only to gain twenty pounds in the process. One habit was traded for another, but in this instance, one is not much better than the other. It's the same thing when we punish a child for something he's done without giving him a chance to visualize and act out an alternative desirable reaction. I'm not saying there should never be consequences for our actions. Consequences are inevitable. What I *am* saying is that we get to mold the child's behavior towards a desired outcome when, instead of uniquely choosing a punishment, such as a detention, we offer the child a chance to write a happy ending to the story. This way everybody comes out a winner.

## He Hit Me!

At some point in our lives, we have surely all taken part in a dialogue similar to the following:

"Brandon, you need to apologize to Jerome for hitting him," instructs a parent or teacher.

"I'm sorry I hit you, Jerome," mumbles Brandon.

"It's okay," offers Jerome, with a noncommittal shrug.

End of story. (Until it happens again...)

When, in the history of humanity, did it become socially appropriate to say to our victimizer that what they just did to us was "okay"? I know what you're thinking: "Kathleen, it's just a manner of speech." Perhaps to adult ears we recognize that it is just a way of saying "I forgive you", but what do the children hear? This is an excellent example of why I believe we need to be more precise with our words. We need to say what we mean and mean what we say, compassionately, of course. Here is an example of how I coach my children and students in forgiveness.

"Brandon, you need to apologize to Jerome for hitting him," I instruct.

"I'm sorry I hit you, Jerome," mumbles Brandon.

"It's okay," offers Jerome, with a noncommittal shrug.

This is where I am compelled to intervene and guide the children in changing their script.

"Are you sure, Jerome? Is it really okay that he hit you?" I ask.

"Well...no," replies Jerome.

"So let's not tell Brandon that it's okay. You need to tell him that, in fact, it's not okay that he hit you, but you forgive him." (Pause) "Go ahead, Jerome. You can do this," I prompt.

"It's not okay that you hit me, Brandon, but I forgive you," repeats Jerome. It is his first time using this language, but a certain air of confidence is discernible.

Addressing Brandon, I suggestively say, "It's very kind of Jerome to forgive you, Brandon, don't you think?"

"I guess," Brandon replies. His vague answer is to be expected. It is an indication that he is unsure of where this is all headed. My goal is for both boys to walk away from this conflict with a sense of well-being. If there is to be any growth, the boys need to feel safe expressing themselves. Therefore, I speak with a firm, confident, yet kind tone of voice, consciously creating a positive energy to ensure an amicable dialogue and a positive outcome.

"Well Brandon," I continue, "I *know* that it is kind of him. It's not easy to look at the person who has just caused us pain and simply forgive him. It takes a certain amount of courage, especially since part of forgiveness is the desire to trust that it won't happen again. How can you prove to Jerome that you are truly sorry?"

Brandon shrugs his shoulders.

"I believe you owe him an act of kindness. Do both of you agree?" I ask the question, knowing full well that they understand there is not really any choice in the matter. However, the act of questioning the boys is a powerful tool, as it forces their brains to process the information in a more constructive manner. They are left in a position where they need to make a choice, and in so doing, commit themselves in a way that is much more empowering than simply being told what to do. The boys exchange a look of understanding and, in that moment, the balance of power shifts to one of equal footing. I am no longer facing a victim and victimizer. Standing before me now are two boys who have been given an opportunity to let go of their pain and to build something positive together.

"Can you think of something you could do for Jerome to prove to him that you are truly sorry?" I ask Brandon. I always give the child an opportunity to come up with suggestions first. Often he will be too shy to verbalize his thoughts, but that does not matter. What matters is that the child sees that I trust in his ability to do something good. It communicates that I have faith in his innate goodness.

"I don't know..." responds Brandon. Considering the fact that this is uncharted territory, it is normal that the child might find it challenging to offer ideas. This is perfectly fine.

"I'm sure you could come up with plenty of ideas, Brandon," I patiently coax. "I've seen you do really kind things for others before." It does not matter if this last statement is true. Words are extremely powerful. As this belief is voiced, Brandon's mind immediately and naturally goes searching for a time when he did something nice for someone else. He is again registering the fact that his goodness has been seen by others. We must never underestimate a child's longing to feel loved. The children who display the most anger or frustration tend to be the ones who have yet to be convinced of the fact that they are worthy of their place in this world.

Turning to Jerome, I ask, "Can you think of something that you would like Brandon to do for you?"

"Maybe he could let me stand in front of him in line?" Jerome suggests, with a sparkle in his eye. (It really is the little things in life, isn't it?)

"There's one idea for you, Brandon," I say, encouragingly. "You could also bring him his lunch box or hold the door open for him at recess." Addressing Jerome, I continue, "So, Brandon owes you an act of kindness by the end of the day. Be sure to tell me once he's done it or if he forgets, okay?" This last instruction is very important as it builds accountability. Brandon knows that Jerome will be reporting back to me as to whether or not he follows through with his act of retribution.

"Okay," Jerome agrees.

"Brandon, you can come and tell me, too, if you like, okay?" I say with a smile. This way, while Brandon understands he is being held accountable, he also sees that he is being trusted to follow through on his act of kindness.

"Okay," agrees Brandon.

The technique of using acts of kindness to prove that a child is truly sorry for what he has done is an extremely powerful one. I have been amazed at how the 'Brandons' of the world will actually perform several acts of kindness towards the 'Jeromes' of the world and eagerly tell me about it. I have even witnessed the 'Brandons' performing acts of kindness towards other classmates as well. When questioned as to what motivated them, they will state it was simply because they saw an opportunity to do so; proving that kids will see what we point their attention towards when done so lovingly. The more we tell children that we see their goodness, the more that they are able to see it for themselves. This is what is known as the "mirror effect" and there is no more beautiful way to put it to use than by telling children just how lovely they are.

It's important to note that I always have the "victimizer" make the commitment to their "victim", not to me. And I ask that they both be sure to tell me about it once the act has been done. I give them until the end of the day, and if ever I forget, I check in with them the next day. When I first put this strategy into practice, I found that the follow-through wasn't there and I rarely heard back from the kids. My mind being what it is, it would be days later before I realized that I had never heard back from either child. Though it's never too late to check in with them, the impact is better within a tighter time-frame. Kids forget. An issue that is huge to them one day can be obsolete the next, which is why it is important to teach the lesson in the moment.

What would have happened if I had gone the traditional, easier route and left things at "It's okay"? Well, everything would have stayed status quo. The balance of power between the two boys would have remained intact. Jerome surely risked a repetition of this type of treatment in the future from Brandon, or anyone else, for that matter, who witnessed the event and the inconsequential outcome. By creating a new dynamic between the boys, they each got a chance to see one another's goodness. Brandon received the message that he cannot go around hitting people without having a concrete price to pay (even if that price is paid in kindness, it is still an obligation he will need to uphold). Meanwhile, Jerome received the message that he is worthy of kindness. That can be huge for the 'Jeromes' of the world who are used to receiving abuse of one kind or another without anyone ever doing very much about it.

Needless to say, both boys were initially uncomfortable with this guided dialogue. At this point in their short lives, they had not often been guided this way in problem solving. Often the victim can be just as wary as the victimizer as to where all of this is heading. Convincing children to participate in peaceful resolution can take some coaxing, but the time I invest in these conversations comes back to me ten-fold in future situations.

It may not be the last time Brandon and Jerome have a conflict, but the groundwork laid out in this conversation will fuel future resolutions. They will have access to the strategies and language that we used and they will need less prompting than the first time.

It is such sweet music to my ears when I overhear one child saying to another, "It's not okay, but I forgive you." This is how we empower our children to stand up for themselves while using kindness and empathy as their guide.

Earlier I mentioned that in order to gain something from the experience both boys needed to feel safe during the dialogue. As we approach situations like these, we must remind ourselves that it takes years of practice to master anything. Pick any one thing you are particularly good at and reflect on how long it took you to hone your skills. Years. Exactly. So how then can we justify some of the common punitive measures that are currently in place for young children? Yes, problems need to be addressed when children misbehave, but too often the message they walk away with is that they are "bad". How is this helpful? If we sincerely wish to reduce violence in our society, we need to analyze our current common practices of how we respond to children when they exhibit undesirable behaviors.

In terms of building our empathy skills, the moment we find ourselves addressing a problem between children and are tempted to say, "You should know better by now!", I want us all to ask ourselves if there is not one thing we did the night before where we should have known better. The difference is, we let ourselves off the hook (or beat ourselves up over it with negative self-talk) because there is no mom or dad hovering over our shoulder anymore, scolding us for reaching for that bag of chips, or lecturing us on how we should have known better than to stay up late watching the end of the hockey game that went into overtime. We must treat kids the way we would like to be treated, and we must guide them in replacing undesirable behaviors with kind actions.

*No act of kindness, no matter how small,*
*is ever wasted*

— Aesop

⌘

# 11

# Teaching Children to Be Kind to Themselves (The Younger Sibling Syndrome)

THE following conversation is an example of how we can teach our children to be kinder to themselves. It is essential that adults be aware of the noise that can be going on in the minds of children. We often underestimate just how critical kids are towards themselves. Reminding ourselves of this can help us to think twice before chastising a child for a minor mistake.

## I'm the Dumb One

Mikella must have been about seven years old at the time. I was hugging her goodnight when she unexpectedly burst into tears, exclaiming, "Why am I so dumb?"

How did my youngest child get to a place in her mind where she believed that she was "the dumb one" of the family? Where did that idea come from? Take a moment to ask yourself what your response would be to your child upon hearing such words. Does the following script match your thoughts, "Oh Sweetie, why would you say that? You are not dumb. Of course you're smart! Don't ever say that about yourself again."

If something like this reaction comes to mind, you're on the right track...but please understand that the train has not yet left the station. This is only the starting point. If we were to stop here, we would essentially be dismissing the child's feelings. If I had just swept Mikella's statement under the rug (because maybe I was too tired or too busy) I would have sacrificed a major opportunity to teach her how to be kinder to herself. Her statement was like a confession. She exposed a wound to me. She made herself vulnerable and gave me permission to assist her in dealing with her pain. This admission had clearly been building inside of her for some time and it took great courage on her part to express her feelings.

The first step was to acknowledge that this statement was true to her. This can be especially difficult for a parent to accept. Nobody in their right mind wants to hear that their child thinks poorly of themselves. It can be tempting to deny the seriousness of such a statement. We may feel our Ego tugging at us, telling us that she's just being emotional or she's exaggerating. Do you really want to risk that?

Mikella is the type of child who is especially private with her feelings. I have a special mantra that I use when I can tell she is struggling with something but too shy or nervous to reveal it. I'll share it with you (please use it wisely):

"The longer you keep your pain to yourself, the longer you are choosing to suffer. The sooner you open up and share about what is hurting you, the sooner you get to release your pain and allow yourself the opportunity to see a new perspective."

This mantra speaks nothing but pure, honest truth. But it only serves us if we use it with integrity. In the moment that we speak it, we have committed ourselves to being open and patient. I believe our heart-to-heart lasted at least thirty minutes. It was late, we were both tired, and I still had one more child to say goodnight to before I could even consider taking a shower and going to bed myself. My True Self had to quiet down my Ego a few times; Ego was saying, "She's just looking for attention," while Self was saying, "She has just laid her heart at your feet. Tread lightly and help her to heal her wound no matter how long this takes."

## How Does One Inspire a Child
## to Rid Herself of Feelings of Inferiority?

Once again, it all came down to naming the fear or the belief that was hurting her. It was akin to aiming a giant spotlight at the false belief in order to see it for the imposter that it was.

"So you believe you are the dumb one of the family?" I repeated back to her.

She nodded her head in agreement as she hugged her pillow tight.

"Mikella, it breaks my heart to know that you think that of yourself. I can tell you for a fact that there is no dumb person in this family. I know for certain that what you say is believed by you, and only you. Your father does not think it, your sister does not think it…" (so on and so forth, as I continued to list family members and friends), "But since you think it's true, we need to look at where that idea came from. Tell me why you believe that."

She began to speak of her older sister's abilities with awe and admiration. She spoke of her frustrations at not being able to keep up with her or to do anything quite as well as her sister could. She expressed her anger at being corrected by her sister for the slightest mistakes. These statements were a reflection of her reality. She shared them with conviction and the pain was palpable. There was a beauty to her vulnerability; it showed the depth of her soul and her longing to be worthy. Gently, without dismissing the truth of her sister's gifts or flaws, I began listing some of the qualities that I observe in her daily. I gave her concrete examples of contributions she makes to the family that are valued and appreciated. I reminded her that her sister was once her age and living and learning similar experiences. And of course, I assured her that I would speak to Yasmine about how to be more of a friend to her rather than trying to mother her.

Most importantly though, I said this: "This family is better and more complete because you are in it. Your soul, your spirit, which comes from the stars, blessed this family when it chose your father, your sister and I to be the ones to share in your journey here on Earth. We are lucky to have you. You complete us. There are no words to express how much we would miss you if you were not in our lives. Pain and struggle are part of growing up. We *will* test each other, we *will* hurt each other, but this is part of the life lessons our spirits are here to learn. Thank you for choosing us to be your guides. Never forget that your soul chose to be the youngest, and that the gifts you share with us are just as precious and valuable as the gifts we share with you. Who knows how old your soul is anyway? For all we know, you could be the one who has lived the most lives in this family. Age is just an idea. Speaking of which, do you see that your sister looks up to you, too?"

"Really? But she's older than me…" she replied, sounding confused.

"Your sister admires you so much. I see it every time she laughs hysterically at your jokes and I see it when she watches you with delight as you show us your new dance moves. She values you and would be lost without you. Think about how far you have come in the past few months. Consider what you could not do at the beginning of this school year versus what you can do now. Can you see how much you have learned? If you keep looking to your sister to measure yourself you will surely continue to feel like you are not good enough -- she has a two-year lead on you! You are not being fair with yourself when you set the bar that high, Mikella. You need to measure *yourself against yourself.*

"By the way, if you think the day will come that you will no longer make any mistakes, forget it! Your father and I are still figuring out this game of life. I still have moments when I think to myself, 'Well that was stupid of me!' The difference is I know that *I am not stupid.* What I did may not have been the smartest choice, but that's okay. Everybody makes mistakes, all the time, every day."

Can I tell you how special she felt in that moment? The glow in her eyes, the softening of her face, and the preciousness of feeling her arms wrap me up in a hug assured me that she had recognized the Truth with a capital "T". Her aha! moment happened for two main reasons, I believe. Not only did she especially enjoy hearing that even mommy does "stupid" things sometimes (that word still has shock value in our home) but also the fact that I used myself as an example allowed her to see me, and *therefore herself*, in a new light. We often underestimate the extent to which children idolize their parents and teachers. When we expose our flaws, children feel reassured about their own imperfections and are more readily able to accept themselves for who they are.

Very little of what I said to Mikella that night was brand new. The thing is, all of our previous conversations inevitably get drowned out by the bombardment of opposing societal values and ideals that come at us every day from all directions. Not to mention that she was a mere seven years old. What's more is that I cannot help but think of a handful of her favorite family television shows wherein each one of the characters are typecast as "the smart kid", "the charming kid" and "the dumb-but-good-looking kid". I cannot come up with one example of a television show geared for children that highlights all of the kids in the family as being equally talented and bright *in their own right*. Perhaps in her young mind, the logical conclusion was that there could not be two intelligent siblings, and since she admires her older sister beyond words, by default, she was the dumb one. This is only a theory, but its implications are frightening. As far as I'm concerned, there is no such thing as a dumb or stupid person, let alone a dumb or stupid child. Every single human on this Earth has gifts to offer the world. Our uniqueness makes each of us intelligent in our own right.

## The Comparison Trap

Maybe comparing ourselves to others is an inescapable phenomenon. How and why some people cast themselves as superior to others while others cast themselves as inferior remains a mystery to me. Is it nature, nurture, or a little bit of both? Either way, empathy, kindness and love serve as our best allies in guiding our children towards a healthy level of self-confidence.

## Do Our Dreams Speak to Us?

When Mikella awoke the next morning she was eager to tell me about her dream.

"Mommy, last night I dreamed I was being chased by zombies," she said.

Oh no, I thought to myself. "So you had a nightmare..." I clarified.

"No, Mommy. It was a good dream," she corrected me. "The zombies were all different colors. I chased them away with the help of some friends and I got rid of them with an exploding bomb," she proudly declared. Wow. I was amazed.

"Do you know what your dream tells me, Mikella? It shows how in the face of something that you used to find scary, you now feel more confident. That's amazing! You did really good work changing your beliefs, Mikella."

She beamed with pride...and my heart breathed a sigh of relief.

"Oh, yeah!" she added, "Plus, the last one had eyes in the shape of hearts and it stared right at me. I wasn't scared at all."

"Could that mean that when we use our heart to see through our fears we realize that there is a lesson we are meant to learn and that we don't need to be scared?" I wondered aloud.

It was her turn to be amazed.

## What Do You Believe?

You decide whether or not you believe that our souls have chosen our families or that there is such a thing as reincarnation. I do not wish to impose anything on anyone. But when the use of such ideas allows us to heal one another in deep, heartfelt ways and when symbolism from the dream of a child can be used to ease fears, I can't help but feel that we are being asked by something greater than ourselves to pay attention. Maybe that ought to be the catchphrase of this book: *slow down and pay attention.*

## Bedtime Heart-to-Hearts

As can be seen in the preceding conversation, one of the most opportune times for heart-to-hearts with our children is at bedtime. In spite of all the hecticness that may have taken place earlier in the day, bedtime is when the energy in the house settles down and we move into a calm space for going to sleep. If this is not a reality in your house, instilling a routine of bedtime chats will likely contribute to a more cooperative climate. My girls look forward to our talks. All I need to do is show up and be present. (Leave your cellphone at the door. This is an interruption-free zone.) As I sit on the edge of the bed, my child speaks. I listen. These heart-to-hearts are about anything and everything, but it always comes down to the same thing. I use these chats to guide my children along the right path. I check in to see that their spirits are whole and thriving; that their souls are at peace.

I have always spoken to my children as if they were young adults, meaning I trust that they can understand regular, adult vocabulary. I may simplify certain things, but I don't dumb-it-down and I am careful to avoid the trap of thinking that they won't understand. Mind you, I don't speak over their heads either. I remind them to ask me about a word if they're not sure they've understood its meaning and I interject new words with synonyms so they have a reference point to guide them. I believe that it is by talking to children in an intelligent way that we ensure they reach their full potential. Kids are capable of understanding so much more than that for which they are generally given credit.

## Never Go to Bed Angry

I am adamant about not going to bed angry, which means that I insist on talking out a problem until we find a resolution. Nothing ought to be so serious that we cannot make peace with one another before we lay our heads to rest.

## Two Questions You Must Answer

1) How important is it to you that you always be right?

2) How hard is it for you to stand your ground with your child?

The answers to these two questions can shed some light on why you may be experiencing problems in the first place. The interesting thing is that we can apply the same solution for either extreme. If in every interaction with your child there is a requirement for *both of you* to be kind with your words then you have won half the battle. Always remember that how you talk to your child is how you can expect them to speak with you: kindness and respect is a two-way street.

## Too Tired . . .

By the way, if you tell me that your child is too exhausted at bedtime to talk, then I suggest you look at implementing an earlier bedtime. If you tell me that's impossible due to all of the activities in which your family is involved, then I suggest you have a family meeting to decide which activities will be put on hold, on rotation, or cancelled altogether. If you tell me that's impossible, then we may have an even more serious problem on our hands than we initially thought because sleep is vital for a child's growth. Brain development, immune system functioning, and healing of bodily ailments all take place while your child sleeps. Please consult the reference section in this book for resources to assist you in solving this problem. You owe it to yourself and your children to have a peaceful home environment, especially at bedtime. Do not underestimate how many common problems today are linked to lack of sleep.

*Educating the mind without educating the heart is no education at all*

– Aristotle

⌘

# 12

# When the Parent Is Too Aggressive

I need to be completely honest and tell you that there are parents who were so unjustly aggressive or rude that, in order to protect myself from their harsh and misinformed criticisms, I stopped communicating with them unless it was absolutely necessary. Since my ultimate responsibility is to the student, putting distance between myself and the parents helped me to continue to view their child through a positive light. Negativity breeds negativity. Parents ought to be asking themselves, "Do I want the teacher to remember this conversation every time she sets eyes on my child? Or do I want her feeling supported and encouraged? Do I want her feeling negative feelings and potentially avoiding my child? Or do I want her to know that, while I may question what is happening in class, I will do everything I can to nurture the idea that she has my child's best interests at heart?"

I'm going to share with you an example of this which occurred a few years back. I had a particularly rambunctious fifth-grade class. They were bright and interesting individuals but, as a group, the dynamic was quite challenging. The majority of them had strong personalities, so the chemistry in the room was such that getting them to listen to each other during group discussions was a constant struggle. After months of trying a wide variety of strategies to teach them how to be better listeners, I decided it was time to appeal to the parents for support. I had each child write in their journal how the group was misbehaving and to list what it was costing them as a class; such as free-time and fun activities. I asked the parents to please speak with their child and to have their child write a response in their journal about what they could do to help make the classroom more peaceful. The journal entry needed to be signed within two days to assure me that the parents had all had this conversation with their child.

I believed that parents would appreciate knowing about an ongoing situation in their child's class and that they would want to support me, the person responsible for their child's wellbeing day in and day out. Needless to say, I was beyond shocked when I received a reply that went something like this:

"I refuse to sign this! I can't believe you would waste our child's precious time in class to write about how some of the kids weren't listening. Maybe you need to find better strategies. If I ever receive a note like this again, I will go straight to the school board to report your lack of abilities as a teacher." (Abbreviated version)

Silly me for thinking that all the parents would see the need for a classroom wherein the kids were required to listen to one another and help keep each other on track. Equally silly of me to assume that all the students would have felt safe and confident enough to be honest with their parents about how they may have been contributing to the problem. The little girl involved in this scenario was not an innocent bystander but she had surely been too intimidated by her parents to be honest with them. This is an example of what I was referring to earlier when I spoke of parents reacting without considering the consequences. I don't think they ever realized the impact that their note would have, not only on me, but also on their daughter and the rest of my students. For one thing, that little girl was so embarrassed to show me what had been written that she pretended to have lost her journal.

My unsuspecting self innocently replied, "How about we go look in your school bag together?" I wish I had the wherewithal to realize why she was avoiding giving the note back to me. At least then, I would have known to wait until the end of the day to read it. Being the trusting person that I am, I had assumed she was scared to show it to me because she had gotten in trouble over it. (Ha! The joke was on me!)

Needless to say, I opened her journal to check for a signature and landed upon the aggressive note I shared above. How could the parents not realize that a note like that can cause serious damage? I was so shaken and hurt. My body began to tremble and I felt myself turn red with embarrassment. I could no longer think straight. My entire being had been sent into defense mode and my ability to take care of my 26 students, never mind teach them the math lesson I had planned, was severely compromised. Fortunately, I had a teacher-in-training with me at the time. She immediately saw that something was wrong and assured me that she could take over the lesson while I took a moment to pull myself together. If the parents were so worried about the quality of their child's education, they would never have dreamed of compromising the teacher's state-of-mind the way they did. Their reaction is an example of how making assumptions can lead to chaos. Thank goodness for the support of my principal who took care of responding to the parents for me. I eventually received a form of apology from them, but I promise you, the way I interacted with their daughter changed from that point on. I made sure I did everything I could to support her, but the only contact the parents received from me in the future was through the use of report cards and general memos. They had made it loud and clear that they did not want to hear about their daughter's behavior ever being anything less than perfect. Therefore, I did my utmost to handle any issues I had with her myself. To be honest, I got the sense that she was grateful for this and I found our relationship improved as a result. The pressure she felt at home to be perfect was more than she could bear and my course of action clearly relieved some of that stress for her. Among other lessons to take away from this is the knowledge that a little bit of fear can be a good thing sometimes. But when a child fears your reactions to an extreme, it is not healthy.

## The Child Must Not Pay for the Parent's Mistake

It's also worth mentioning that I spoke with their daughter alone afterwards to see what she knew about the note. Her mother's handwriting being difficult to decipher, she actually did not know what had been written, just that her mom had been very upset with me. She and I spoke about the journal entry, and I had her articulate to me why the message *was* important and what her role had been in contributing to a difficult situation. She admitted that she had been too scared to be honest with her parents. So she and I struck a deal. So long as she would take my warnings to get back-on-track seriously, I would not see any need to communicate with her parents. Only if she were to test my word unreasonably would I then take the route of calling or writing her parents. This deal worked really well for the both of us. Now I know some teachers would say, "Hell, no! Those parents need to know their child *does* create problems in the classroom. If you never contact them again, then they're left thinking they were right!"

My reply to that reaction is simply, "Don't let your pride get in the way of what matters most." Consider the Core Principles of communication. The purpose of communicating with the parents ought to be to help improve the child's success at school, not to convince them that whatever techniques you choose to implement are correct. Sometimes it is best to agree to disagree, and sometimes we make this decision quietly on our own. In so doing, we refuse to fuel the fire.

The parents showed me that they lacked good judgment when they sent that note off in the first place. I happen to know that it was written the night before, too, so not even a good night's sleep was enough to help them see how their emotions had run wild and that they were being unreasonable. I *could* have contacted them in order to try to convince them why I felt my discipline strategy was appropriate, but would this really have been the best investment of my time and energy? A wiser choice, and the one I made, was to inform my principal of their unkind letter and to request that he speak to them on my behalf. (This is yet another advantage of teaching through kindness: your principal is likely to appreciate the fact that building positive relationships is a priority for you, and he is likely to reiterate this to parents when he communicates with them on your behalf.)

We must never lose sight of what matters most: the students. They are, and must remain, our number one priority. If I have the parents on-board with me, that's fantastic, and their child has that much more of a chance to thrive as a learner. But if the parents have shown themselves to be unkind, unfair, egotistical, or just downright bullies, I need not concern myself with them unless it is absolutely necessary. If ever I do see the need to communicate with them, I do so in person so that the principal can be present at the meeting, as well.

There is no way I am going to set myself up to be bullied by anyone, especially not a parent. It bears mentioning that these parents were never rude to me again and when they were faced with a situation for which they needed to contact me, they were quite humble in their approach. It would seem that my silence, coupled with my principal standing up for me, had spoken volumes. The message had been received.

That day was a significant moment in my life as a teacher. It's around that time that I began learning how to live by the following two mantras:

**We teach people how to treat us.**
and
**Fool me once, shame on you.**
**Fool me twice, shame on me.**

It also bears mentioning that every other parent in the class signed the journal entry without any complaints. In fact, several parents thanked me for letting them know what was going on and to be sure to keep them informed if matters did not improve. A couple of parents even took the time and energy to acknowledge that their child was part of the problem and apologized on their behalf. Overall, the strategy was rather effective, yet in spite of my 96% success rate, I never again repeated it quite the same way. I have never been willing to risk being abused like that again. Yes, I know; nothing is personal. I sincerely believe that in my heart and soul. However, it does not change the fact that harsh, accusatory words hurt, and it can take time to process and digest them; time I do not have when I am responsible for teaching the 26 students sitting before me in my classroom.

The next time you feel like sending a harsh letter or email, first ask yourself if it is actually helpful. What is motivating you to voice your thoughts, and what is your desired outcome? By choosing to practice empathy, if not towards the teacher because you are too angry, then at least towards your child and his classmates, you will truly be leading by example with kindness. This way, you will be ensuring that the lessons of that day are taught as planned. Not convinced? Ask yourself this: Do you want to be responsible for the teacher abandoning a lesson involving an engaging hands-on science experiment because your words were so accusatory that she lost her ability to focus and teach? Your words can directly impact the teacher's state of mind. How you choose to relay a concern can, and will, make a difference for everyone involved.

As for me, I learned an important lesson on empathy as well. I had not considered the idea that some kids let loose in class because they have very little room for personal expression at home. Maybe this group needed to be loud and expressive. Maybe there was just no way around it.

## Moving Forward

In the future, I will be applying the following mantra to all that I do:

**Make every decision based on the best people.**

- Todd Whitaker

In his book, *What Great Teachers Do Differently,* Todd Whitaker explains that teachers ought to ask themselves, "How will my best students feel as a result of my decision?" In so doing, we are often compelled to take a different approach to discipline. I am certain that my best students were not thrilled about writing that note in their journal. I would have loved to have excluded them from it, but it's impossible to be sure that somebody who was acting up wouldn't have slipped through the cracks. To be fair, I had to assign the task to the whole group. And yet the truth is that it still wasn't fair, even if I was counting on the best students to explain the story properly to their parents. If I had asked myself, "Who is most comfortable and who is least comfortable?", I surely would have come up with another plan. For instance, they could have glued the following note in their journal :

Dear Parents,
Hello! The students and I have been working hard at communicating appropriately with one another by practicing listening without interrupting and by learning how to take turns in a conversation. Therefore, the homework for the next few nights is to have conversations as a family where everyone practices these skills. You are free to discuss anything at all. Please be sure to ask your child to describe the dynamic in the classroom during conversations and have her tell you what she thinks could be improved upon. I would like your child to make a brief journal entry about the experience. Also, I would greatly appreciate it if a

parent could write a comment about their experience in the journal to say how this activity went. I hope you will find this homework enjoyable! I know it is a little different from the norm, but communication skills are a big part of the curriculum and I felt the children could benefit from some extra practice.

This action would not only have made the best students feel comfortable, it would have even given them the chance to vent their frustrations about how some kids in the class are really lacking in this department. The parents who are involved and who care about their child's behavior in class would have easily understood the reasoning behind this assignment and would, hopefully, have had an important conversation about classroom behavior with their child. And for the minority of parents who do not pay much, if any, attention to their child's progress, this note would have simply gone unnoticed; but so, too, would have the journal entry. Basically, the kids who would have had very little feedback to offer would likely be the ones who had good reasons for being disruptive. These are the types of kids who lack attention at home and who will get it any way they can at school. For these kids, either note would not have had the intended effect of making them uncomfortable because they know their parents won't do anything about it anyway. It is not to say that we simply give up on these kids, but we have to realize that they tend to be used to punitive measures and most have already developed a certain immunity to them. Teaching through kindness, however, allows us to speak to their hearts. The students who fail to return this homework are the ones with whom we get to have a special heart-to-heart one day at recess or during quiet reading time. The lack of response from home becomes an opportunity to better understand their reality and to reiterate why it is that we care so much about instilling good habits in them. And, if as a result of all of these efforts, we notice that positive changes are taking place in their self-control, then we should take the time to send a letter or email home to parents congratulating the students for the improvements that we are noticing in class as a result of the homework assignment. An encouraging letter home is bound to have a positive impact on our students. (Be sure to read it to the students first!) Perhaps the parents who struggle to show enthusiasm or support towards their child's education are not used to receiving positive feedback. Who knows what this type of letter could do to effect a positive change in their views towards school? It is always worth a try.

*Have a heart that never hardens, and a temper that never tires, and a touch that never hurts.*

– Charles Dickens

⌘

# 13

# Is It Funny or Is It Rude?

MY youngest daughter is especially witty. She has been experimenting with sarcasm since she was at least five years old. I can think of countless times when her quick-witted response to a seemingly adult situation has caught us off-guard...but in a good way. There's a sense of pride that comes in witnessing our children's linguistic abilities developing at an impressive rate. The trap we can easily fall into, however, is if we continue to measure future comments and reactions by this same bar or level of ability. We can forget that a child's learning is much like Swiss cheese. There are sure to be holes in their comprehension that have yet to be filled in.

I'll never forget the day when, at the tender age of five, Mikella "mouthed off" at me. Though I cannot remember her exact words, I do recall the emotional reaction it brought out in me. I suppose you could call it "the straw that broke the camel's back". She had been a little too snarky for my liking in the weeks leading up to my outburst, and I had been thinking a lot about how my parents would never have tolerated half of the comments coming out of her mouth. So when she said to me, in a sarcastic tone, something to the effect of, "Yeah, right...You think I'm going to pick that up, but I don't think so!", I lost it. Phrases akin to, "Who do you think you are, speaking to me like that?" and "How dare you be so disrespectful?", followed by, "Go to your room! Now!" came streaming out of my mouth at a voracious pace. "It's time she realizes who the boss is in this house," I thought to myself.

The look on her face will probably never leave me.

"What did I do wrong?" she cried. "Why do I have to go to my room? I didn't mean it!" she begged.

I remember just looking at her, as my past and present realities merged together as one. The belief systems constructed in my childhood came crashing up against Mikella's expression of shock and pain. The old beliefs in my head were telling me, "Don't be ridiculous. Of course she knows she's wrong. Take charge and teach her a lesson in respect." Meanwhile, a much kinder and more empathetic voice was whispering in my head, "Look at her properly. See beyond the words and look into her eyes. She is in pain. She is sincerely confused."

The assumption I was making in that moment was that she knew exactly what she was saying, and that she knew she was wrong. My beliefs about the appropriate way children should behave, and my fear of allowing inappropriate behavior to get out of hand and lead my child astray, caused me to react strongly. What if I were to make a kinder assumption? What if, instead of being certain that she was intentionally being rude, I entertained the idea that she doesn't actually know what she is saying? In so many ways I wish I had gone this route in the first place, but since I believe we must live without regrets, I am grateful for the lesson this confrontation taught me.

As it dawned on me that she very well could be telling the truth and that it was possible she did not comprehend the depth of her wrong-doing, I forced myself to change direction. Of course, my old system of beliefs challenged me on that as well, "Don't let her break you! It does not matter if you're wrong about this, she can still be punished for being rude, whether she meant to be or not." (This may be a good time to mention that my father's father was a military sergeant, and so strict adherence to the rules was a major focus of my upbringing.) The kinder, softer voice in my head gently reassured me, "It cannot hurt to talk this out. Try to gain a deeper understanding of your daughter and the way her mind works by allowing her to explain herself. You have already made your point. She definitely sees she did something wrong. Sending her to her room will only serve to alienate her further. Your Ego may be feeling proud of the fact that you took control of the situation, but the truth is if you leave it like this, you will only succeed in severing a line of communication and trust with your child." I've elaborated earlier in this book on the primordial need to build the lines of communication with our children while they are young and receptive. If we wish to have teenagers who will be open with us, we need to use every chance we get, when they are young, to prove to them that they can trust us to listen.

As love presented itself to take the place of pride and Ego, my face softened and my voice took on a note of compassion. Looking her in the eyes I said to her, "I feel like you are telling me the truth and that I don't need to be this angry." A shift in her defensive stance was immediately visible. "I am telling the truth," she replied, her voice cracking as the tears streamed down her face.

"Ok, Mikella, I believe you. I'm not angry anymore. Let's talk about what you said. Let me teach you what it was about it that upset me so that you don't find yourself upsetting someone else in the same way."

Together, we turned an unpleasant event into a teachable moment. In more ways than one, my daughter learned about the power words have to hurt, but more importantly, the power they have to heal. As for myself, it was an awakening to the realization that we must not automatically assign an adult perspective and understanding of an inappropriate word or phrase to what is spoken by children. Language is a living organism. Children and adults alike are constantly building their repertoire of words. The meanings of words and expressions take on new depth and significance as we use them with those around us.

When I questioned her motives, I came to discover that I had misinterpreted her words. She informed me that she thought she was being funny. When I analyzed what she had said, I saw how that could be true. How many times in the past had we laughed at her perfectly placed, witty remarks? It made me realize the extent to which, each time a child tells us a joke or a story, they are actually in the midst of building their understanding of language. The desire to communicate a creative or original idea is integral to the human existence. As a child shares his tale, he is noticing his audience's reactions and taking notes. We can compare it to a toddler who accidentally trips over his own feet and, noticing his dad's spontaneous laughter, chooses to repeat the action on purpose in search of that same pleasing reaction. In the infamous words of Charles Dickens, "There is nothing in the world so irresistibly contagious as laughter and good humor." It is human nature to seek out the joyful sensation of laughter and, more often than not, a rude or snarky comment from a child is often just a failed attempt at a joke.

## While We're on the Subject of Humor . . .

We must not underestimate the extent to which our children are influenced by media and popular culture. As they watch television shows, view blockbuster movies, and stream video clips, they are naturally learning what gets a laugh and what doesn't. They are absorbing the various intonations used for the delivery of a joke. And then they try it out themselves. If you, as a parent, laughed at a snarky comment in a show, how can you blame your kid for imitating it? They want to make you laugh, too. Laughter is one of the greatest joys in life. We all know that sinking feeling when we tell a joke and it doesn't get the reaction we hoped for...and we're adults! Kids are developing their sense of humor in accordance to what they are exposed to. When we make this connection, we are better equipped to empathize with our children. It helps us to reevaluate our reaction to a seemingly rude comment and allows us to guide them in their comprehension.

Some of you may be thinking that if we are constantly giving our kids a chance to explain themselves then we are teaching them that they can talk their way out of being "in trouble" for something they've done wrong. Keep in mind that the idea of punishing our kids dates back to an authoritarian style of parenting – one I believe we ought to be steering away from as much as possible. The trick is to find the balance. Of course, our children will try to pull the wool over eyes. They *will* try to manipulate us into getting their way. But I think that if we are paying attention and we aren't the type of parent who thinks our child can do no wrong, then we will know when this is happening and we will handle it appropriately.

When we see that their protests are nothing more than an attempt at making excuses, we will call them out on it...all the while congratulating them for their cleverness! (Humor has more than one use.) Rather than being focussed on "catching" them when they mess up, why not just seize teachable moments and talk it out? Maybe I'm biased to this approach in part because I am quite sarcastic by nature, but I find discussing things with a hint of humor makes life way more enjoyable. Moreover, I'd prefer to leave my child feeling like there was a positive outcome to an uncomfortable moment, rather than a negative one. While a negative outcome can have a more lasting impression, since the child may want to avoid feeling that way again, a positive outcome fuels my child to be confident when she speaks rather than fearful of making another mistake and being unjustly reprimanded.

Ultimately, we want to raise children who know how to make their way in this ever-changing world. When we guide them in being responsible for their actions without being overly punitive, I believe we set them up for success. We give them the confidence to take chances. Our children will express themselves the best way they know how. And when they mess up, as all humans do, we can correct with kindness instead of harshness.

*The most wasted of all days is one without laughter.*

– e. e. cummings

⌘

# 14

# Question Assumptions

WHOEVER proposed the idea, "Never make assumptions," really missed the mark. "Never say never," I say. Assumptions are a natural and indispensable part of the human existence. They help us to make sense of our world. Our brains are designed to categorize information, and the only way to do so effectively is to judge what we see and assume that we have judged correctly. This strategy helps us get through our day. It is even possible to view assumptions as an act of faith and trust. When I pull up to a red light, I trust (or assume) that the car behind me is going to stop. When my daughter brings home an empty lunch box, I assume that she ate all of her food. When my boss tells me he appreciates the work that I do, I assume that I should keep doing what I am doing. Assumptions are a means of drawing conclusions and they help us choose how to react in any given situation. They are not inherently bad.

Since none of us can truthfully claim that we never make assumptions, it's time to replace this inaccurate notion with a more appropriate belief. I propose the following:

## Always Question Assumptions
## That Give You a Dramatic Emotional Response

The assumptions we make that leave no real impression on us are probably fairly accurate, or at the very least, harmless. So long as our assumptions do not create any pain or conflict, then we can probably leave them be. (There may come a time when a seemingly harmless assumption proves to be wrong, but we can deal with that when the time comes.) It is when our assumptions create noise in our heads that we need to pay attention. If a situation brings about a strong emotion, then empathy and kindness need to be called upon for assistance *before* we trust our reaction. Too often, we can feel so sure of our judgment of a situation, and act on our beliefs, without fully entertaining other possibilities. We can get easily confused, thinking that we are helping by coming to someone's defense, without properly questioning the other side of the story.

**Your assumptions are your windows on the world.**
**Scrub them off every once in awhile,**
**or the light won't come in.**

– Isaac Asimov

Consider the following common scenario. A child, let's call him Trenton, comes running up to you. "William said I'm mean!" he cries. He is clearly agitated and hurt by the unkind words spoken about him. I cannot begin to count the number of times I have dealt with this type of accusation. A typical, familiar response in this situation might be, "You go tell William he hurt your feelings," or "William, that's not nice! You need to apologize." While these types of responses are well-meaning, they do very little in terms of helping Trenton to understand what's actually going on inside of him. To truly help him, and to turn this into a learning experience, we need him to question his reaction by speaking to his heart, not just his mind. We must help him see that he has just made an assumption and that in order for William's accusation to be so upsetting, a part of Trenton *had to actually agree* with William.

When Trenton came running up to me to tell me about William's accusation, my first step was to leave William out of it. I would speak with William later. My priority was to help Trenton make sense of his feelings.

"Why would William say that about you, Trenton?" I ask him in a neutral voice.

"He says I pushed him to the ground, but I didn't! I was running and I bumped into him."

"So William assumed you knocked him over on purpose, but you want him to understand that it was an accident?"

"Yeah, but now he thinks I'm mean!"

"Is he right?"

"No. It's not fair that he said that. It's not true."

"How did you react, Trenton? Were you calm and did you kindly apologize right away? Or did you get angry and defensive when he accused you of being mean?"

"...I got angry, but only because it wasn't true!"

"Do you want me to let you in on a little secret, Trenton? The only person who ever really *needs* to know the truth, is you. When *you* know the truth, you do not need to get upset at all. Since you know what really happened, you can stay calm and apologize wholeheartedly. I know it doesn't feel fair that he accused you, but by getting angry in return, it makes it seem like you have something to hide and that you aren't telling the truth. Accidents are going to happen. When people see you staying calm and sincerely apologizing, then it is easier for them to see the truth."

I can tell from the look on Trenton's face that he is trying to work out what I have just told him. I cannot expect him to grasp everything I've said. I call this planting seeds. So long as I have made him consider a new possibility, I have done a good job.

"But what do I do now? He thinks I'm mean!"

"Is it true?"

"No."

"So prove it. Your actions speak louder than words, Trenton. Go out of your way to be extra kind to William and say sorry to him like you really mean it. That ought to be enough for him to see that you were not trying to be mean. Haven't you ever wrongly accused someone before? This is a chance for you to think twice about your own reaction the next time something like this happens to you. It's also a chance for you to question if what other people say is true, especially when it's unkind. We can't control how someone else is going to treat us or react to us. We can only control how we respond to them. You have to admit that it is fair to expect someone could be upset when they suddenly get knocked to the ground."

"Yeah, I guess that's true."

"Okay, let's go see William together to clear this up."

As I approach William, it is clear he has been expecting to see me. As I address him, my goal is to disarm him.

"Hey, William, are you alright?", I ask in a mildly concerned voice.

At this point, William has had time to realize that he overreacted and that it really was just an accident. Otherwise, Trenton would not have wasted his time in getting a teacher involved. My next step is to model the generosity of spirit that I wish to inspire in both of them when future misunderstandings occur.

"I'm fine," William responds in a quiet voice.

"It seems Trenton really surprised you when he accidently knocked you to the ground. Are you still angry about that or is it okay now?" Notice how I used the word "surprised" to neutralize what happened, followed by the choice to no longer be angry. Phrasing it this way gives William the opportunity to let go of his feelings without the sense of having lost a battle. Children do not always realize that they have the option to let go. Providing children with reasonable choices is an effective strategy which can be used to resolve countless conflicts.

"It's okay," William replies.

"Do you know that Trenton feels really bad about what happened? He wants you to know he really wasn't trying to being mean. Did he apologize to you?"

"Sort of."

"Did you maybe get a little too upset with him?"

"Maybe…"

"Thank you for your honesty, William. Neither one of you meant for this to happen. You were both surprised and didn't react in the best way. It happens. How about we both clearly and calmly say sorry about what happened to each other and we can put this behind us."

I love watching the transformation on children's faces as they realize the truth. The ability to empathize exists in all of us. We need only call attention to it and it will appear. The more we cultivate it, the more harmonious our daily interactions with others will be. We cannot help the fact that our Ego is typically on the front lines, ready to defend us. It is the Ego's job, after all, to keep us safe. There comes a point, however, when we can catch our Ego before it takes over, and learn to be more generous and empathetic in any given situation.

Now, some of you may be thinking that I put an awful lot of thought and effort into something rather trivial. I beg to differ. Unless something major suddenly happens to which you need to switch your attention, neglecting to take the time to give these boys tools to resolve a small conflict, in an empathetic and peaceful manner, would be a missed opportunity. Conflict resolution courses are great, but nothing serves anyone better than real life experiences. It is when we are in the moment that we can bridge the gap between theory and reality.

Accusations are so easy to make and children are often quick to jump to conclusions. Could this be, in part, because they are mimicking the adults in their environment? If more adults could learn to address these types of situations in this spirit, I sincerely believe we would witness a dramatic decrease in bully-type behaviors. We would create a new, healthier version of "normal" for our children.

*If you know yourself,*
*then you'll not be harmed by what is said about you.*

– Imam Sufyan Al Thawri

⌘

# 15

# Positive Motivation

WHEN it comes to motivation, empathy is our greatest ally. People want to know why they need to do something. It's an innate desire and, as Simon Sinek explains in his Ted Talk entitled *How Great Leaders Inspire Action*, it's actually part of our biology. "When we communicate from the inside out (beginning with "why", then "how", then "what") we're talking directly to the part of the brain that controls behavior." In order to help a child see "why", we must put ourselves in his shoes in order to see the reason for which he is resisting our instructions. We must learn to see through his eyes. Doing so enables us to connect with the child. When a child feels heard and understood, then, and only then, do we have any hope of making some kind of significant impact on him. This is what I believe Nelson Mandela meant when he said, "If you talk to a man in a language he understands, that goes to his head. If you talk to him in his language, that goes to his heart."

Allow me to elaborate. As adults, we tell kids our stories and expect them to grasp the lesson. We're confused when they don't seem to care. Yet somehow we forget that we did the very same thing when we were kids. How many times did you secretly (or overtly!) roll your eyes every time you heard your dad say, "When I was a kid…".

We need to learn to tell our stories in a new way if we sincerely wish to be heard. We can't just hit them with, "When I was a kid…" and expect them to be all ears. Somehow, someway, we need to capture their attention by making them see that we do, in fact, have a sense of what they are going through.

And before we start to preach, we better be prepared to listen. It's not until we have invested a great deal of time simply listening to *their* stories, *their* concerns and *their* reality, that they will even begin to consider the possibility that we may have some helpful advice to offer.

Nothing impresses my daughters more than when I say, "Sweetheart, I can't pretend to know exactly what you're going through. Can I tell you what I think might help? I'm not saying this advice will be perfect, but maybe at least a part of it will be useful to you. You can decide what you want to do with this advice, if anything." The discovery of this "disclaimer" was like finding gold. If the mood is light, another script that works well is, "I know it's hard for you to imagine because I am so old now, but I was once your age…"

Like most kids, my daughters want to fix their problems by themselves. This mantra has been my gateway into being able to support my daughters without them feeling like I'm taking over or that I'm telling them what to do. (Of course, it works well with my students, too.)

## The Wrong Crowd

Let's look at the following scenario for how we might apply the principles of motivation. Remember, we are trying to see the situation through the eyes of the child. But in order to see their motivation, we must first analyze our own thoughts and assumptions. You will notice throughout the conversation that I am asking a lot of questions which all boil down to "why". Rather than jumping to conclusions, I am digging as deep as I can, in the limited time that I have, to get to the heart of the matter.

Anita is a woman I see every now and then at the gym. She approached me the other day. "I know you're a teacher. Perhaps you can recommend other high schools to me? My daughter is fourteen and she has landed in the wrong crowd. She has just failed two of her classes and she doesn't seem to care. All she cares about are her friends and talking about her hair, her clothes, and boys. And she's always on that darn phone of hers! Maybe if she changes schools, she'll get serious."

"I have yet to raise teenagers, so whatever advice I have to offer, please take it with a grain of salt," I began. "First, let me ask you, do you truly believe her behavior will change in a new school?" I asked.

"You know, my daughter said the same thing when I told her I would change her school. She says she's a follower and so she'll just end up with the same type of girls, or worse," Anita confided.

"I find it interesting that she sees herself as a follower. I'm not accustomed to hearing kids label themselves as such. I wonder how authentic that statement really is or could she be using it as an excuse for her behavior?" I replied.

"I was thinking the same thing...You know, she doesn't care any more about trying to get an 80% on a test. As long as she passes with a 60%, she's happy. How can she can be fine with that? I need her to care more...How can I make her care more? Two weeks ago when she failed those two classes, I took away her phone and she has yet to get it back. I don't know what else to do."

There was so much more I needed to know before I could be of any service to this loving mother. It was clear as day to me that she cares about her daughter. My gut was telling me, though, that her daughter was feeling alienated from her right now and that the disconnect was having a downward spiral effect.

"Has she always done well in school? Is it unusual for her to be struggling?" I inquired.

"I have a tutor for her. I know if she just works hard enough, she can do it," Anita stated in a matter-of-fact tone.

The certainty in her voice rang alarm bells for me. "She's currently enrolled in the international program though, right? That's a program that has great benefits, but is it possible she is feeling overwhelmed by the increased workload?" I pressed.

"Her cousins are always on the honor roll. But she just doesn't seem to care. She doesn't even try."

"This may not be what you want to hear, but I can't help but feel that for most of the kids who are on the honor roll, it comes relatively easily for them. What looks like a wonderful accomplishment is actually a reflection of their passion or their natural aptitude. By no means am I discrediting those students who put in hours of hard work to be on the honor roll, it's just that, in general, the school setting is designed for a specific type of child. Those are the children we tend to see on the honor roll. It's not fair to expect every child to fit that mold. If every child achieved it if they 'just tried hard enough', it wouldn't even exist, or the criteria would change. The design of the honor roll, in my opinion, is flawed. It separates students based on 'school smarts' but neglects all the other areas that the so-called 'regular' students may thrive in. It sounds to me like your daughter is the type of child who has talents that do not fit the mold of the school system. Am I right? What is she passionate about? What does she imagine herself doing later in life?"

Anita's face lit up as she began describing her daughter's love for animals and talent for architectural design. Needless to say, neither of these domains are focused on in the first twelve years of school, which can easily lead a child to believe that school is pointless. Through the art of asking "why", we had finally dug deep enough to uncover what might be the root of her daughter's lack of motivation. We finally had a golden nugget with which to work and I was ready to offer some advice.

"Here's the first step I would take if I were you, Anita," I advised. "Set aside some time for a heart-to-heart with your daughter to ask her about her passions and her dreams. You need to find some common ground and rekindle a friendly connection. Have her tell you what she sees herself doing in the future, then research college and university programs to see what the prerequisites are for these programs. Give her some concrete information as to why passing her classes with decent grades, not just scraping by, will enable her to attain her dreams. Explain to her that she needs to have good grades to get accepted into the program of her choice. At this point, she just doesn't know any better. She has no tangible reason to care. By getting on board with her dreams, and seeing things through her eyes, you may be able to give her the motivation she needs to work harder."

Anita was keen on giving this a try. I was curious to know how her daughter was handling not having her cell phone so I asked, "Have you noticed any improvements in her behavior since you took her cell phone away?"

"...Not really, no," Anita admitted.

I had a theory as to why it might not be having the effect for which she had hoped. "Does she know what she needs to do in order to get it back? Have you negotiated some type of a contract with her?" This had not occurred to Anita, so I elaborated, "It's possible that your daughter sees no reason to apply herself harder in her studies because she has no hope for regaining a piece of her independence, that is, her phone."

"She is crazy about her phone!" interjected Anita in agreement.

"Most fourteen-year-olds are, right?", I concurred. "It might help to sit down with her and negotiate a written contract as to what you expect of her if she wants to get her phone back. She needs to realize that her cell phone is not a right, it's a privilege, and she needs to know exactly what she must do in order to have access to it." Anita liked the sound of that idea, so we left the conversation at that.

A few days later, our paths crossed again. The expression on Anita's face was all I needed to know that she had succeeded in getting through to her child. She explained to me how her daughter was surprised to learn of the requirements for college acceptance, specifically those related to architecture. It was the equivalent of flipping a switch. The next day, this fourteen-year-old girl approached her science and technology teacher to sign up for remedial support. As for the cell phone, Anita was still holding on to it but her daughter was thrilled about the idea of a contract. They had yet to pin down the exact criteria, but good grades, not just scraping by, were definitely at the base of the agreement.

"I can't believe how quickly I was able to get through to her just by changing the way I was saying it!" Anita shared with me.

"It all comes down to re-framing the situation. You are still delivering the same message, but in a way that she can understand. You are speaking *her* language," I explained.

"That's exactly it!" Anita agreed. "You know, I feel bad about the way I am using her phone to get her to work harder. It feels like blackmail. But she loved the idea of a contract, so I guess I shouldn't feel bad..." she added.

"It's not blackmail, it's positive motivation. You are teaching her about the real world and natural consequences. That phone is like money to her. Just as we have to work to get a paycheck, she needs to do her work to get her phone. There's no difference and it's a valuable lesson on the importance of having a good work ethic," I assured her.

*We either make ourselves miserable*
*or we make ourselves strong.*
*The amount of work is the same.*

– Carlos Castaneda

⌘

# 16

# Fresh Starts

I'M a big lover of fresh starts. When we don't like the path we are on, we have the power to press a reset button. If we want kids to learn how to make better choices, we must show them that we are capable of doing the same. It is essential for adults to reflect on how they react towards incidents and to establish whether their reactions are helpful or hurtful. When the adult realizes that he could have done a better job at conveying his message, he must take the time to acknowledge it. In so doing, a precedent is set for the child. It can be as simple as a parent telling his child what he plans on doing differently and to keep reminding himself of this "choice to change" when he sees his old reactions popping up. Fresh starts can be challenging, but I believe they are an intrinsic aspect of choosing the path of kindness first. I'll give you an example.

Anyone with young children knows how difficult it can be to maintain a clean home. I have always been the kind of person who likes things to be clean and tidy and I was determined to be the super mom who could do it all. As much as I was familiar with the expression, "Don't sweat the small stuff", it was easier said than done. In spite of how patient I can be with many things, I would sometimes witness myself overreacting to something as trivial as a glass of spilled milk. I wouldn't be able to hide the irritation in my voice as I insisted that they be more careful and pay attention. The popular saying, "Don't cry over spilled milk" would play in my head and I would feel guilty about my reaction. I came to realize that my obsession with desperately trying to keep a spotless home was hurting my children. It was not very compassionate of me, nor was it a realistic goal if I didn't want to lose my sanity.

For one thing, it's not like I never spill or break anything. Second, I realized I was not actually making my kids a priority when I was spending more time cleaning the house than playing with them. The day my house will be spotless, it will also be empty, and I'm certain a part of me will miss the crumbs on the floor and the smudges on the mirrors - symbols of a family life.

These days, I am much more relaxed when something breaks or spills. When I first changed my reaction, I could see my girls cringing, waiting for me to get upset. That's when I realized that I needed to tell them about my choice to change: "I know I used to get upset over these kinds of things but I've realized it's not a healthy reaction. I prefer to be relaxed about it now." The smiles that would spread across their faces as they heard these words were all I needed to know that I had made the right choice. It can take several incidents and many reminders to ourselves before we manage to break the old conditioning and replace it with the new, more relaxed version, but I promise you it's worth the effort. Don't be surprised at yourself when you slip into old habits, either. That's to be expected. Just catch yourself, own your behavior, forgive yourself, and move on.

## First Impressions Matter

While parents need time to prove to their children that they are changing how they do things, teachers have the advantage of starting fresh each fall with a new group of students. One of the most effective ways to nip problems in the bud is to not really expect any in the first place. Instead, I focus my energy on letting the children and their parents know what kind of behavior is expected. The beauty lies in the fact that whatever I expect of them is exactly what they can expect from me. As I set limits for myself, I simultaneously set them for all the other people involved in this ten-month journey.

The first day of class is always exciting and nerve-wracking. I have yet to sleep soundly the night before I meet my new students. First impressions matter. I'm not talking about the impression they'll make on me. I'm an adult, so I know better than to take any of their potentially challenging behaviors to heart. I realize that by the time they arrive in my care, they already have dozens of preconceived ideas, feelings and emotions about school. For all the anxiety I feel, I can only imagine what some of them are going through. For all of these reasons and more, I greet my students with an open-hearted smile and make eye contact with each and every one of them as they choose a seat. Once they are seated and I have their attention, I begin my introductory speech.

"Welcome to third grade! I can only imagine how each of you is feeling. Many of you are excited; others are nervous. Some of you love school and are thrilled to be back, others may not be very happy about being here. I can understand that. My ultimate mission is to make each and every one of you feel excited about school. Absolutely everybody has a special gift or talent to share with the world.

"Now, there may be someone here thinking, 'She doesn't mean me, though.' Yes, I do! Everyone, especially you! You may not have discovered your gift yet, but I promise you, you have one, if not several. This year, each day will be filled with new opportunities to discover our strengths and our talents. School is not always easy, but the challenges can be fun if we choose to look at it that way. You must always feel safe to ask your questions. You are in a space that tolerates nothing less than 100% respect, kindness, and open-mindedness. It is by being a risk-taker that each of you will grow in your learning.

"I'm sure you know of teachers who believe in being very serious with their students. They don't smile or tell jokes for at least the first month or two of the school year. I suppose they believe this is the best way to show the students who is in charge. Maybe that works for them but I do not see things that way. To me, every day is a gift for which we ought to be grateful. We will be spending five days a week together, morning until afternoon. As far as I'm concerned that makes us a family, and when I'm with my family, I like to feel happy, joyful, and relaxed. I will greet you every day with a smile. I will exercise patience and use a firm tone of voice when giving directions to correct behavior. I wish I could say I never lose my patience. I wish I could say I never raise my voice. The fact is, I'm human and I have emotions, too, just like you. No matter what though, I promise to always be my best, even if my best is not always the same from one day to the next. I ask the same of you. When I make a mistake, I will apologize for it. Pobody's nerfect, right? (pause) Get it? PO-body's NER-fect?"

I always give them a moment for the play on words to sink in. Eventually, as comprehension dawns on a handful of children, they spontaneously volunteer their understanding to the rest of the group. "Ooooooh, Nobody's perfect! Hahaha!" I love this moment so much. The joke may not be that funny, but the intention is understood. As laughter and smiles spread throughout the room, the positive energy that is connecting us to one another is palpable. This talk sets a precedent and a standard for the year. My message is clear: I care about being a caring teacher, and I care about them feeling comfortable in this space. They instantly feel more relaxed just knowing that humor and laughter is not only welcome in our class, it's a must.

To wrap everything up before moving on to our next activity I tell them, "I am so looking forward to getting to know each and every one of you. I sincerely believe that each of you has been brought into my life for a reason. In fact, we are all in each other's lives for a reason. We will all have things to learn from each other this year, of that I am certain. I see it as a privilege to be given the chance to be your teacher and I promise I will teach you to the best of my ability. All I ask in return is that you promise to be your best as learners, which means showing up in class with an open mind. I am really excited about this year!"

In case you haven't noticed, I am really proud of this speech and I think I have good reason to be. It has taken me years to refine my balance between caring and having a loving approach while being firm and setting high expectations for both myself and the students. I am 100% convinced that this is the healthiest route to take with children. We should not be waiting for children to show us respect before they gain it from us. We ought to offer it and demonstrate respect to them so that they have a proper example of what it looks like. We need to stop assuming that children should know better. Maybe they don't. Certainly, we are all able to conjure up images of adults being rude and even mean to children. If the majority of the adults in a child's life have been better at preaching than teaching (i.e. do as I say, not as I do) then be grateful that you have the opportunity to be the best role model yet for this child. What an amazing privilege. Consider the place you will hold in that child's heart knowing that you may be the first adult to truly connect with him in a kind, loving and respectful way.

The more we resist the person who stands before us, the more likely we will struggle indefinitely with him. Whereas the better we become at accepting a child as he is, the more likely we will be able to effect positive change in his life.

## Teach the Child First

I have heard teachers say, "We're expected to be therapists these days. I went into teaching to teach." If, as a teacher, you love your subject more than your students, you may want to reevaluate your choice of profession. There is nothing more important in the classroom than the people. It starts with the children. They must be at the center. It is imperative that teachers do everything in their power to ensure that each of their students feels liked by them. It is a huge error to disregard the importance of having a positive relationship with each student. A child who senses that he is not liked by his teacher will not be engaged as a learner in the same way as the one who does feel liked. Notice that I am not saying you must actually like all of your students. Sad as that may sound, I can concede that some children are so wounded that they can be difficult to like. In spite of this, and even because of this, you must make the child feel liked by you. Find something, anything, about the child to like and focus on that. You may be surprised with what you find. You may also be surprised by how much you end up liking him for real! As a parent, if you sense your child feels disliked by his teacher, you owe it to your child to discuss your concern with the teacher. How? You can simply say to the teacher, "My son is feeling quite insecure these days. Can you make an extra effort to show him how much you like him?" This way you are not implying that the teacher does not like your child and you are simultaneously paying attention to a potential problem.

*If you judge people, you have no time to love them.*

– Mother Teresa

⌘

# 17

# The Defiant Student on Day One of Class

DEPENDING on the school you find yourself in, you may have anywhere from a couple of very challenging students to an overwhelming handful. (If it's almost the whole class, then just go ahead and adjust the following script for the entire group.) I typically have a handful of challenging students each year and here is how I proceed. I do not single the child out in front of the others if I can help it. (I can almost always avoid singling a child out. A dangerous situation may make it unavoidable, but it can still be done with tact.)

As soon as I get a glimpse of defiance, I seize upon it as my opening. I will invite the child into the hallway while the others are busy doing their work and I will say, "Do you know how happy I am to have you in my class this year?" This usually prompts a look of surprise. "I mean it," I continue, "I was really hoping I would get the chance to be your teacher." I don't have to tell you that a child who exhibits defiant behaviors in school is not prepared to hear this from his new teacher. He is expecting me to be upset or to give him a stern warning. He does not necessarily believe what I am saying, but I am certain he wants to.

Word travels fast in a school, so I usually already know which students may be behaviorally challenging. Since I already did my homework, I know a bit about this child. I pick one or two things that I've observed, or that a previous teacher has told me about, and I let him know that I value his skills. For instance, I may say, "Last year, I overheard you joking around with your friends in the hallway. You have a wicked sense of humor. I hope that you will make us laugh in class from time to time," or perhaps I'll say, "I hear you're quite good at soccer. I can't wait to see you play at recess."

Basically, I use this time to bond with the student by letting him know that I believe in his goodness or that I see his talents. Then I get real honest with him. "Look, I'm sure you know that I know that you sometimes get in trouble at school. It's not like it's a big secret. I'm not too worried about that because I have a really good feeling that, together, you and I are going to find ways to help you change your bad habits. As far as I'm concerned, I believe that most negative behaviors are just bad habits that need to be switched out for good habits. I am going to be respectful and kind towards you and I'm confident that you're going to be happy to treat me the same way. Together, we'll find strategies to make sure that your habit of getting in trouble gets turned around into something positive. What do you think?"

Each time I've had this chat, the reaction is quite similar: the child is clearly surprised that I had something good and kind to say to him. If you or the student are new to the school, don't worry. You just need to be creative. With a little observation you can surely identify something to build a positive connection on between yourself and the student. Even a simple comment about the style of his hair or the funky color of his shoe-laces is a step towards building a relationship built on mutual respect.

It's not always going to be easy. With my toughest students, I usually tell them that they remind me of my brother, my sister, or even myself. By connecting them to a member of my family, they receive the message that I see something in them to which I can relate. My goal is to let them know that they can expect something different from me and that I see their goodness. Up until now, thanks to some (possibly unintentional) negative reinforcement from key players in their lives, they have been cast into an unfavorable role. My mission is to offer them a new, positive role. I let them know it is safe to try out new behaviors. For instance, to the child with a great sense of humor, I tell him that we will work on learning how to choose his timing to tell jokes in class. The class clown is not just welcomed, but appreciated, and we all congratulate him when he gets his timing just right. (We also let him know when he misses the mark, but we do it kindly.) To the child who is quite active, I let him know that I admire his energy and we find ways to channel it constructively.

I promise you that if you believe in this approach, it will work. I am not saying you won't work just as hard, if not harder than ever, with these children. The difference will be in the energy each of you experience as you work through difficult situations. There will often be joy, laughter, and smiles...if not at the start, than at least by the end. Empathy and kindness will assist you in gaining and maintaining a cooperative attitude with your students. You will have more fun in your classroom. The times when you do resort to raising your voice with them, you will get an amazing response. They will care about your reaction. They will know that you are not speaking forcefully simply because you enjoy the sound of your voice. They will know that they have pushed it too far and they will adjust their behavior accordingly. They will even apologize sincerely for having gone off track. They will do this spontaneously because you will have modelled it for them time and time again.

When you do use a tougher tone, here's what you will likely be saying, "Have I not been kind enough towards you so far this year? Are you showing me the same kindness? Have I not made it clear that if something is bothering you then there are other ways to deal with your frustration? I am nothing but patient and kind to you. I expect the same in return." If you've been speaking with just one student in the hallway you'll continue by saying, "I'll be back when you are ready to speak with me properly and to take responsibility for your actions. Right now I am too upset to speak with you."

I'll leave the student alone in the hallway to reflect. When I do return, I am calm, but I only engage him in a conversation if the child is calm as well. Otherwise, I walk away again. In so doing, I set my limits. I will not engage in a battle with a child. That would be pointless and a total waste of time and energy. I know because I've been there, done that. All it ever accomplished was that I would go home with a headache and I'd be full of toxic energy. Worse, it chipped away at the trust I had built with the student. Without trust, there is very little left to motivate a child to be his best.

Am I as happy as I say I am to have especially challenging students in my class? Yes and no. The truth is, I am nervous. Nobody wishes to have a class full of behavior problems. But my belief is that the child with these problems is struggling to find his place in the school environment. Some of it comes down to maturity, and some of it comes down to his need to be truly seen and appreciated for who he is. His behavior is an indication that he does not have faith in the classroom experience, and probably for good reason. These are the children for whom the system has not been designed. I make it my mission for him to know that I will do everything I can to adapt to his needs, but he will need to make compromises as well. I will not always like everything he does and he may not always like everything I do, but my actions are always motivated by love.

Every child needs to know that they are accepted for who they are. We are all innately good. Many behaviors do not fit into the accepted norm but many of them can be used or redirected in order to turn them into strengths. Though children may need to learn how to manage their energy and their attitudes, teachers need to learn to adjust their expectations (and attitudes, too).

## Why Is This Better than Doling Out Punishments?

At first, being caring and empathetic takes more time and energy than simply bullying children into behaving. But what are we teaching them when we threaten to remove their recess or give them extra homework? What are we teaching them when we choose to threaten them?

That teachers don't care? That their feelings don't matter? Children are not just going to walk up to us and say, "You know Miss Tatiana, I woke up to the sound of my parents fighting, so I stayed in my room longer than usual, which means I was late and I didn't get to eat, and since I was rushing, I forgot my gloves so my hands are so cold it hurts. That's why I'm in a bad mood and I'm having trouble concentrating this morning." For some kids, a difficult start to the day can be the norm. What are we teaching these children if we resort to threats and punishments? They need to know there is a safe place available to them every day. That is our professional responsibility.

## Safe Zone

The gravest error we can make as teachers is to think for even a second that we can disconnect the emotional human being from the learner. I do not pry into the details as to why my student's morning routine is miserable. That is none of my business. However, teaching children to honor their feelings, and guiding them towards being the best they can be in spite of their circumstances, *is* my business. The number one rule in our classroom is that everyone gets to feel safe and welcome. By setting up a classroom that allows children to eat as soon as they arrive in class, they do not need to explain if or why they are hungry; they can take care of their needs without the discomfort of admitting to a problematic morning. By reminding children that, for the duration of the day, they can choose to forget about their home life and it's problems, and that here, in this class, they will be spared from being screamed at, we set up conditions for learning.

Before anyone gets upset, I am not accusing parents of being cruel or abusive towards their children. Nor would I ever say anything of the sort to my students. I am simply stating the fact that not all families are living a fairy tale life. The systems I put in place in my classroom are designed to create an environment that makes every single child feel comfortable, safe, and cared for, regardless of their situation at home. Moreover, while my students know that they can count on me to listen to their problems and to care for their needs, I believe they appreciate knowing that I will not probe into their daily lives (unless something alarming indicates to me that I should.)

Teachers, never forget that yelling at your students can be more damaging than you realize. For the children who are growing up in a relatively peaceful home, they may be able to tune you out. But for those who are living in conflict or complete mayhem at home, you are destroying them. And please don't play dumb on the issue. Hands down, the kids at whom you most feel like 'blowing your top' are almost always of the latter group, and you know it.

Parents, if any of this sounds familiar, then I beg of you to make changes in how you deal with your problems. If you honestly think that screaming and arguing does not affect your child, you are dead wrong. As much as I encourage students to leave their worries at the door, they do not all succeed in doing so. I have watched children suffer silently at their desks. I have wondered about what is wrong, and I have often come to learn, one way or another, that something is going on at home. We all have problems. We will all explode with emotion now and again, but ceaseless fighting is detrimental to your child and you must find solutions. Ask for help if you need it. An integral part of teaching kindness first is being the example for your child. Words have no meaning if the actions are not modelled.

*The greatest thing you'll ever learn, is just to love and be loved in return.*

– Eden Ahbez

⌘

# 18

# Meeting Fire with Fire

LIKE it or not, sometimes we need to meet fire with fire. Typically, I only raise my voice when I have made at least three attempts to get through to a misbehaving child calmly. Once I do raise my voice, my words are clear and direct, as always. *It is never okay to insult a student.* Never. You can raise your voice and be forceful with your words if necessary, but never do you belittle them. You judge the sin, not the sinner. You require him to own his actions, but you make it clear that his actions do not define who he is. They are learned behaviors that need unlearning. That child needs to know that you believe in his ability to do better.

What would a conversation like that sound like, you ask? The following incident took place in the schoolyard with a group of sixth-grade students. It's not always perceived as "cool" to ask for help, so when I noticed Derek discreetly waving me over to where a bunch of them were horsing around and sliding on a patch of ice, I knew something had to be up. As I drew nearer, I could hear a bunch of them telling Timmy, another sixth-grade student, to "Cut it out!" and "Wait your turn, someone's going to get hurt!"

I arrived just in time to see Timmy throwing himself on the ice and crashing into Billy, another student who happened to be half his size, and who had yet to get out of the way. Billy burst into tears from the pain. Those standing around exploded at Timmy in protest. "We told you to stop! What's wrong with you?!" they accused. They weren't wrong. In fact, I was impressed with how they had been looking out for each other.

Derek immediately went to Billy's aid, and as the two headed inside to take a look at Billy's ankle, I caught Timmy's eye and asked him to come with me. He immediately launched into his defense, "It wasn't my fault! I didn't mean to hurt him! He was in my way!"

"Timmy, the others were clearly asking you to wait your turn. You didn't give Billy the time he needed to get up and move out of the way," I replied in a low, steady voice.

"I didn't hear them! They just don't want me to play with them!" he protested.

"Timmy, they want to play safely. For sure they're not going to want you there if you're not willing to cooperate," I explained. I was still calm at this point.

"Walk with me," I gently instructed. I distanced ourselves from the group in order to give us privacy and to make sure I wouldn't be overheard saying anything that could embarrass Timmy. I was also hoping that my calm disposition would be contagious. With many kids, this technique works really well, but Timmy clearly didn't have the awareness to pick up on my lead.

"Oh my gosh! This is so unfair!!" he yelled.

Timmy's inability to follow my cues was my indication that he was unable to speak my language. He didn't have the tools. I needed to meet fire with fire.

Raising my voice and looking him straight in the eye, I firmly explained, "No, Timmy, you're wrong! I'll tell you what's unfair! What's unfair is purposefully throwing yourself on the ice knowing full well that Billy could get hurt. You're twice his size. Don't you realize you could have seriously injured him?"

"It wasn't my fault!!!" he screamed.

Meeting fire with fire means there will need to be a storm before the calm. I had expected him to get more agitated. As much as I dislike confrontation, I knew we were headed in the right direction. Raising my voice even louder and speaking with greater force, I retorted, "Are you kidding me? If you're going to yell at me, then I'm going to yell at you! Can't you see I'm trying to help you? I was calm this whole time, but you had to keep pushing. You are not the victim here! Billy is! We're going to the office. Let's go."

Timmy started to cry. "Good," I thought to myself, "The tears are a sign that I have broken through to him." (Never let tears scare you. They are a language unto themselves and need not be feared. They especially should not make us cave in and lose sight of the real problem.)

We entered the school in silence. Once I had him seated in the office I told him that I needed a few minutes to calm down and that I would speak to him when I felt ready. I informed both the principal and his teacher of the incident, since at this point he was missing some class time. (It would have been senseless to send him back to class. Being present in body would not make him present in mind; not to mention the reaction from his peers that awaited him. His teacher needed a chance to smooth things over with the group first.)

Seeing that he had calmed down, I sat with him, and in a gentle voice, I explained, "Timmy, I did not enjoy getting angry with you back there. Do you realize that at first I was trying to get through to you peacefully?"

Timmy nodded his head in agreement.

"I was not looking for a confrontation with you. Rather than being willing to take responsibility for your actions and apologizing, you felt the need to defend yourself. My very first words to you were calm and understanding. I get that we all mess up sometimes. My goal was to help you smooth things over, but you could not hear me. I only managed to get through to you when I joined you in your anger, and that's a shame, don't you think?"

"I know, but they're always picking on me because of my size," he told me.

I didn't doubt the sincerity of this statement but I would not allow it to throw us off the current topic. "Timmy, I believe you. Kids can be mean and it's not okay. But in this scenario, your size posed a threat to their security on the ice. It was not necessarily a judgment. You could have seriously injured someone. And do you honestly think that by acting the way you did, you would somehow convince them to be nicer to you?"

"I don't know," he replied, sounding discouraged.

Of course he didn't know. Timmy is an overweight, twelve-year-old boy living in a society that is disturbingly obsessed with being thin. My heart went out to him, but he would not get my pity. I'm not into pity. I'm into empowerment.

"Timmy, I will speak with your teacher about them teasing you about your weight. That's not cool. But let me ask you this: do you think the kids picking on you are perfect?"

"What do you mean?" he asked.

"What I mean is that nobody teases someone else unless they feel badly about themselves. Someone who truly loves himself only wishes to be kind to others. Those who are picking on you are doing it because they know it bothers you, but also because it makes them feel better about themselves. Don't tolerate their teasing. Call them out on it," I advised.

"Find enough love for yourself that you can accept who you are, present weight and all. Clearly, your size bothers you, otherwise their comments would not hurt you. If you want to lose some weight, your teachers and I can help you come up with a plan to make healthier choices. First though, you need to love yourself the way you are, inside and out. You're a kid, Timmy. You are just figuring out that the habits you have are not serving you. They are not allowing you to be the person you wish to be. But all habits are temporary. You have the power to make any changes you want."

I realize that's a tall order for a twelve-year-old, but he needed to hear it from someone. I was not going to let this opportunity pass without trying to have a positive impact. In that moment, he was my student, even if he was not in my class. If I succeeded in planting a seed of hope for him, then I did good. Before I left him to go back to my students, I said, "Timmy, I hope you know how much I care about you. If I didn't care, I would not have put this much energy into trying to help you. I hope you'll trust me next time to be able to talk with me without getting so defensive."

"I know, Miss Kathleen. Thanks," he replied warmly.

What an emotional journey that was. I know we don't always have that much time to invest in situations like these. It was lucky that I didn't need to get back to my students right away after the recess bell. Sadly, time constraints often keep us from being able to have these valuable heart-to-hearts with students. It's worth noting that before I made the choice to take this path with Timmy, I had asked myself whether or not I had the time to see this through. It would have caused more harm than good to engage in a heated conversation with him if I didn't have the time to teach the lesson of peaceful resolution at the end.

For the rest of the school year, when Timmy and I would cross paths in the hallway, he would greet me kindly. The warmth in his eyes was enough to reassure me that I had chosen the appropriate course of action with him. I don't kid myself into thinking that I worked some kind of miracle that day, but I do know that I had a lasting, positive impact on this boy; and that is worth every ounce of energy that I poured into those twenty minutes with Timmy.

Kindness is not to be confused with weakness. It is strength. It is giving someone exactly what they need in any given moment, in spite of how it makes you feel. It is having faith in the notion that when your motives are anchored in love and caring, you are doing the right thing. If there is one thing that situations like these teach me, it is that life is far less black and white than I ever could have imagined.

*Tell me and I'll forget;*
*show me and I may remember;*
*involve me and I'll understand.*

– Xun Kuang

⌘

# 19

# It's Not Personal

AS hard as it is to put into practice, I sincerely believe that nothing is ever personal. Everything is always a reflection of someone else's reality. This is an idea put forth in Don Miguel Ruiz's book *The Four Agreements*. It's a book I highly recommend. I have been rereading this book at the beginning of each school year for years now, and I have gifted it to numerous student teachers with whom I have had the pleasure of sharing my classroom. I believe we spend too much time pointing fingers at the one who did something wrong and not enough time reflecting on how the victim could react differently. I'll give you an example of what I mean. I'll name the boys Peter and Luke.

Every classroom has at least a few 'Peters' and 'Lukes'. Peter and Luke are the type of kids who could not be more different if they tried. These two do not like each other and they are pretty upfront about it. Peter comes from a home that practices and models kindness. Luke, on the other hand, comes from a home where screaming and name calling is the norm. Peter cannot understand why Luke is often loud and rude. He finds him offensive. Meanwhile, Luke cannot understand why Peter gets so upset anytime he calls him a name or yells at him. From Luke's perspective, Peter is overly sensitive and he needs to toughen up. Do you see where I'm going with this? They do not understand each other because they are not even remotely living the same reality at home. Our initial understanding of the world, and the meaning we create from that understanding, comes first and foremost from home. When all of these varying realities are thrown together into one classroom, let alone one school, is it any surprise that we end up with so much conflict?

I may feel tempted to get involved by speaking with the parents, but I need to tread carefully. I have legal obligations to report suspicions of abuse to the authorities, but I cannot impose parenting styles on people. There is a fine line between parents who believe in authoritarian practices and those who are actually verbally abusive. I can hope that they will read my book and pull lessons from it, but I cannot assume that all parents are interested in my opinion. I offer it only when asked, and I do so with tact.

Fortunately, though, I am Peter and Luke's teacher, so not only can I teach them how to appreciate one another, I believe it is an integral part of my job. Each time these boys approach me to help solve a conflict, my first step is to resist focusing on the actual complaint. I'll address it briefly and then move on to the heart of the matter. A play-by-play of "who-said-what-to-who-first" will rarely ever be accurate anyway. What matters most is how each of these boys are feeling about what happened and the self-talk going on in each of their minds. Typically, no matter what happened, the 'Peters' of the world are busy feeling hurt and thinking about how unfair it is that Luke was mean to him and the 'Lukes' of the world are annoyed because even though they may know what they did was wrong, they have no idea why this has to be such a big deal.

The first thing to keep in mind is that we ought to give the bulk of our attention to the perceived victim. Upon receiving a complaint, we often have a tendency to launch into lecturing the accused. While we're busy seeking justice for the victim, we are actually fueling the victimizer. Essentially, he was looking for attention. If we zone in on him first, well, he got what he wanted. Kids who are used to negative attention will thrive on any kind of attention at all.

Now, pay close attention to what I mean when I say we must address the victim. I do not mean that we feel sorry for him. When I say we need to get to the heart of the matter, it means we are going to question Peter about why he feels hurt. As I often do, I ask Luke to go take a few minutes for himself so that I can speak with Peter alone.

I say to Peter, "Why do you think Luke's words bothered you?" By no means am I blaming the victim for his problems, please hear me out. If I were to say to Peter, "Poor you, Luke was mean to you again. Let's get him to apologize," all I am actually doing is contributing to Peter's view of himself as a victim. Sympathy and empathy are not synonyms.

My goal is to give Peter the chance to reflect and look within himself. Peter is likely to tell me that he believes it's mean to yell and call someone a loser. I can then agree with him. More than anything, all Peter really needs is to have his feelings validated. He is right to say that it's wrong to call someone a loser. It is not kind or helpful in any way. What Peter does not realize is that Luke is used to being called a loser. For Luke, there is very little shock value to this word or any other words like it. It's his everyday language. So I carefully explain this to Peter, always using the art of questioning, which forces Peter to really think about what I am saying.

"Peter, do your brothers or your parents ever call you names?", I ask.

"No," he replies, an expression of confusion visible on his face.

"Are you able to imagine that maybe Luke is used to being spoken to this way from his family?", I suggest.

"Really? Well, actually, yeah, I guess. He's always saying how mean his brother is to him." This realization inspires Peter to feel a spark of compassion for Luke. He can't imagine his brother or his parents ever speaking that way to him.

"Are you able to see that you are the lucky one, Peter? As hurt as you feel by Luke's words, can you imagine how much he is hurting? He's so used to this type of language that he can't even see that it isn't normal or right."

By offering a better understanding of why Luke acts the way he does, I empower Peter to detach himself from Luke's actions. I help him to see that Luke really doesn't know any better, even if we think he should. (Keep in mind, confidentiality rules always apply and we must not divulge personal information about our students to others. In this particular case, Luke had already made public statements about how things are for him at home, therefore I was simply helping Peter to connect the dots.)

"I am not excusing Luke's behavior," I continue, "But knowing that this is his reality can help you to see what I mean when I say that nothing is personal."

## Teaching the Victims That They Need Not Be Victims

As Peter gets better at not believing the words that are spoken about him, he begins reacting differently to Luke. Instead of feeling hurt by Luke, he feels compassion for him. He sees Luke's pain and he can better appreciate how lucky he is that he does not go home to a house that tolerates such language. He wishes Luke could live in a home like his where no one would ever dream of being that mean to each other. This is not pity. Pity breeds feelings of superiority. This is empathy. Peter has imagined himself in Luke's life and he does not envy him. He realizes that the pain he has felt from Luke is only a glimpse of the pain Luke lives with regularly. I teach Peter to tell Luke, "I won't talk to you that way, ever. We can be friends and you can trust that I won't be mean to you." This may sound unlikely but I promise you, I've seen it happen and it is such a joy to witness.

As for Luke, the journey is obviously longer and harder, which is another reason why it's important to teach the 'Peters' of the world that nothing is personal. Meanwhile, Luke gets a different form of guidance all together. I expect him to apologize, but not in the way you may think. His apology comes in the form of an act of kindness towards Peter (as I discussed in Chapter 10). Luke wants to be seen as kind and he doesn't know how to break the cycle of being seen as a bully. There are real bullies out there, but I believe there are far fewer than the statistics claim. Luke is not a bully. Luke is a child who has not been given enough opportunities to do the right thing and have it be noticed.

Now that I've finished taking care of Peter, I call Luke over for a private chat. When I address the issue of Luke's hurtful language, he is quick to pass the buck. "My brother talks to me like that all the time. Big deal," he says.

"I believe you when you say it's normal to you, Luke. I don't believe you, though, when you say it's no big deal," I reply.

"Whatever. Everybody talks like that. Peter is just a baby," he accuses.

"Actually, Peter is not used to being spoken to like that at all, Luke. That's why it hurts him so deeply. When he leaves school, he goes home to a relatively peaceful evening. He and his brother get along really well and his parents treat each other respectfully."

I share this information with Luke compassionately. I see the sadness in his eyes as he takes in this information. I have just confirmed for him that he's right to feel angry and hurt by the way he gets treated at home. It may seem like I am being callous by pointing out to Luke how Peter has it better than him, but quite the opposite is true. I am giving him the opportunity to choose better for himself. By knowing that a happier option is possible and actually exists, he can imagine that future for himself and eventually break the cycle of pain.

I continue, "Luke, I get why you're angry and I get why you lash out at others. I wish I could make your home life more peaceful. Maybe, as you get older, you will be able to teach your family some of the lessons that I am teaching you. Until then, what I can do for you is create a classroom that only allows for kindness and understanding. This way you have a place to go to every day where you know nobody is going to call you names or yell at you. It means you get to let your guard down and practice treating others the way you wish to be treated. Also, you can trust that they will return the kindness because I will not accept any less from anyone in this room. This is what I have been talking about all year when I say, first and foremost, that we must take care of each other." (Now imagine what will happen when this expectation is upheld not just by individual teachers, but as a schoolwide or boardwide philosophy... wow.)

There are at least two important negative consequences to simply telling the 'Lukes' of the world that their actions were hurtful and they need to "say sorry". First, the 'Lukes' are confused. They usually have parents or siblings who are treating them this way all the time and no one seems to have a problem with it. How are they supposed to react? How does a child go about changing his behavior when the primary people in his life act this way towards him on a daily basis? Second, we wind up teaching the 'Peters' of the world that when our feelings are hurt, it is the other person's fault. While that may be a common belief in our society, I believe any pain we ever feel is a result of our interpretations. Again, nothing is ever personal.

## Prove That You Care

I won't lie to you. As I am writing this story my eyes are welling up with tears as the faces of all the 'Lukes' I have taught appear in my mind's eye. My heart breaks for these kids. They are on their way to being the bullies of our schools and our workplaces unless the people on the front lines do something about it. They need compassion. I am not talking about giving them permission or excuses for their behavior. I have major *tête-à-têtes* with the 'Lukes' of my life but all of my words always come from a place of love. I tell them, "I care about you. I believe not only in your ability, but also in your desire to do better and to be better. I would not put all of this energy into correcting your behavior and showing you a better way if I did not care about you."

My most challenging students have heard me say on more than one occasion, "You exhaust me! I am completely drained...and I refuse to give up on you. If you think you can just push me away, you are sorely mistaken. If you think you can be so mean to me that I will just give up, you are wrong. I care too much about you. I care more than you can imagine. I *will* get you to understand and to trust me when I say there is a better way for you. Do not underestimate *my* patience and *my* stubbornness."

I am not delusional. I know I will not "fix" all of my students' challenging behaviors. But I will hold my ground and stand up for what's right. As my dad used to say, "Pick your battles and when you do, make sure you win."

## Remember to Care for Yourself

If all of this sounds like a lot of work, you're right. It is. I give more love and more empathy to my students than I ever thought was possible. It can be draining, but there are ways to minimize and even reverse the exhaustion. For one, the more positive I remain in my techniques and strategies, the less drained I feel. It's also really important to not take my students' actions as a personal attack on me. Teaching requires a lot of energy, there is no question about that. However, the more negative thoughts I allow myself to think, the more tired I am and the more likely it is that I will wind up ill from the stress. The less I allow myself to get caught up in negative thoughts, the more vibrant I feel.

A couple of years ago, a friend of mine convinced me to start going to the gym at least three times a week. I was sure I did not have enough time for that type of commitment. He assured me I did and he urged me to give it a try. It turns out he was right. Even just thirty minutes of running or dancing on the treadmill is enough to refuel me. I'm usually exhausted when I step on the machine, but I leave the gym feeling more energized and more alive than when I arrived. Not only is the gym an outlet for some of my frustrations and stress, but it's like a reset button which allows me to go home feeling calm. My husband and children can attest to the positive impact this has had on the entire family. For me, the gym has been my saving grace. For you it may be a stroll in the forest, scrapbooking, or baking. Find your "gym" and make time for yourself. Nobody can give the best of themselves from an empty cup.

> *Nothing other people do is because of you.*
> *It is because of themselves.*
>
> – Don Miguel Ruiz

⌘

# 20

# Sensitive Boys

IN the previous chapter, we looked at how a teacher might support a child in distress. However, the reality for a parent can be quite different. Though the parent knows his child better than the teacher, the history and dynamic between a child and his parent can actually make it more challenging to solve a problem. Not to mention the fact that the parent does not have all the information. He is forced to deal with issues outside of the environment in which they took place. It can be an onerous task. As heart-breaking as it can be to see a child in pain, we can take solace in the fact that they are able to feel their emotions. The best thing we can do is honor their feelings. Would we discourage a child from laughing whole-heartedly at one of our jokes? Why, then, do we have a tendency to hush away their tears? When we acknowledge a child's feelings, we help to remove the embarrassment or shame he may be feeling.

I want to mention that I have intentionally chosen boys for these scenarios in order to draw attention to the stigma associated with boys who cry easily; which is, sadly, still quite present in our society. It's no secret that I do not have a son, but I'd like to think that my experience within the classroom is sufficient to be credible. As far as I can tell, boys cry just as much as girls, but the bias in accepting tears from girls more than boys is still very much seen and felt. My mission here is twofold: I wish to teach these sensitive boys to honor their tears and to teach all of my students that we have no right to judge someone's pain. My personal experience with tears is that when we stop feeling embarrassed by them, and we understand them as a physical expression of our thoughts, it gets easier to accept their presence. In his book, *The Language of Tears*, psychologist Jeffrey A. Kottler speaks of the value of encouraging tears. He draws our attention to the point made by Nico Frijda that it may help to adjust our beliefs when we consider "that crying doesn't so much express sorrow or helplessness as it *is* these feelings in behavioral form."

Let's consider the following scenario. You are sitting at the dinner table when your son bursts into tears. How do you react? Are you comfortable dealing with tears or do you have the urge to make the crying stop? No matter the thoughts that are going through your head, you must have the wherewithal to press pause, look at your son, and listen. It is essential that you open with a question and not a statement, since a statement could easily be interpreted as a judgment or an assumption.

Looking at your son, you begin in a calm voice, "Joey, what's upsetting you?"

He may be unable to tell you right away. If that's the case, do not push the issue, but speak with confidence.

"Okay, Joey, I trust that you will tell us what's bothering you once you're ready. If it takes you all the way to bedtime, that's fine. Just remember, we have an agreement that it's important to not go to sleep upset."

This reaction communicates a variety of things to your son. For one thing, you are letting him know you respect his feelings and his privacy. You are not asking him to deny his feelings, nor are you belittling them. Whatever is bothering him is big for *him*; whether or not you will agree with his evaluation of the problem is irrelevant. You will get your chance later to inspire a different perspective. Secondly, you have given him the gift of time. He can sit with his feelings a bit longer, allowing the worst of it to pass. Simultaneously, you have subtly informed him that he will have to talk about it before the day is done.

In the meantime, your message to your son is simple. You say to him, "Let it out. Tears are healthy. They release toxins from your body. If you want to leave the dinner table for now, that's fine. Or if you just want us to change the subject, that's fine, too." He may be too upset to talk at all. If that happens, here's a little trick you can use to lighten the mood and change gears. You are not making fun of his feelings. You are acknowledging that it is too hard to talk in the moment.

You can say, "Nod your head once if you want us to ask questions until we figure out what's wrong. Nod your head twice if you want us to just change the subject and have a completely different conversation."

If he gives the one nod, make some genuine attempts to figure out the problem. Consider the issues he may be facing at school or difficulties he may be having with his siblings, for instance. If after several attempts you make zero progress, that's when a little humor can work. This is when you can make some ridiculous comment like, "A dinosaur barged into your room and stole all your toys! Where is he?! I'll teach him a lesson!" Tell the joke gently, looking for eye contact, in an attempt to lighten the mood.

Humor is a tool that, when used properly, can ease the pain of any situation. By this I mean that you are careful to make a joke that is totally implausible so as to not risk belittling the actual problem. No one knows your child better than you, but in my experience, if he gets even more bent out of shape when you try to make a joke, the problem he is dealing with may be bigger than you initially thought. Tread carefully. Hopefully, your child relaxes and breaks into a chuckle. This is an indicator that he might be ready to share. Your joke has empowered him in the sense that he realizes you are trying to understand, you are ready to listen, and you are calm and receptive.

Never underestimate how nervous a child can be about opening up about a problem because he fears that you may overreact or that you may try to take control of the situation. Often, a child just wants to be heard. He may want help to find a solution, but that doesn't mean he necessarily wants you to solve the problem for him.

Let's assume your son has waited until bedtime to talk about his outburst. As you dim the lights, and tuck your child in bed, you gently say that it's time to talk. It still may take a few minutes for him to speak. If this is the case, you can say, "I love you too much to let you go to sleep holding onto this pain. I'm not leaving your side until we speak about this. I may not be able to fix the problem for you, but I can at least share the weight of it. Keeping it to yourself is hurting you. When you let it out you will feel lighter just knowing it isn't stuck inside of you anymore."

It may take a few more minutes, but a message such as this one ought to be enough to convince your child that it is safe to open up about what is hurting him.

Joey confesses, "Adam called me stupid."

How should you react? In your head, you may be thinking, "That's it? Big deal!" This is definitely not what you should say. Your primary goal is to honor your child's feelings and guide him to a place where these words won't hurt him anymore. Here is what you know about Adam. Joey and Adam have never really been friends. Joey is a sensitive child who is kind to other kids. Adam is a boisterous child who sometimes lashes out at others. Your best course of action is to respond with a question to force your child to work through the thought process himself.

"Do you think he's right?" you ask calmly.

Joey is quiet as he considers your question. "No…", he finally replies. There is a discernible hesitation in his voice.

"It seems to me that part of you must agree with him if you're this upset about it," you suggest.

Joey responds in protest, "I'm not stupid!"

You knew that this would get an emotional reaction from your son. That's okay. You will disarm him by saying, "I know that you're not, but do you? Anytime anyone says anything about us we have a choice to agree or disagree with them. The trap in life is that we often like to hear nice things said about us and so we're quick to agree with that person. But what happens when someone says something hurtful? We're already in a pattern of agreeing with what people say about us, so we believe it, too, even if it hurts us."

"Well, he's wrong. I'm good at a lot of things," Joey asserts.

"I agree," you reply, "Tell me some of the things you're good at."

Prompting Joey to name his qualities will be more meaningful than you telling him. However, if he seems stuck for examples, you can get the list started for him. Once you have established some of Joey's strengths, it's time to give him a strategy for the future.

"The next time someone says something hurtful towards you, try to take a second to think about what they have said before you react. Ask yourself if you think they're right. Your self-talk could sound something like this, 'I know I'm not perfect, because nobody is, but I don't deserve what he just said to me.' When you realize you don't deserve it, then you can move on to feeling empathy for him. A reply such as, 'I would never say that to you so please don't say that to me,' can go a long way in making a kid realize that you are not going to take his abuse."

While the scenario I offered is a common one, I mentioned the very real possibility of having a much more serious problem. What if Joey reveals that a child has been repeatedly taunting and teasing him. What if it has been going on for weeks, even months, and he has kept the whole thing to himself? Resist jumping to conclusions. We must be careful with the over-popularized term "bully". Remember, Joey has not told anyone about this problem until now. His "bully", therefore, has not been spoken to yet and has not had the opportunity to change his behavior. The "bully" needs help, too. We must seize moments like this to either establish or reiterate core family values such as, "The bigger or more serious a problem feels, the more important it is to tell a parent." It is also why I stress the importance that nothing is personal. When we teach children to recognize that they always have control over their own beliefs and reactions, and that they can put themselves first in a loving way, we empower them. Kindness is not just for others, it is for ourselves as well.

## Food for Thought

How we teach our children, especially our boys, to deal with their emotions is exactly what I was referring to in the Chapter, "Start as You Mean To Go". Let's ask ourselves, "How are we raising our boys? What kind of men do we wish for them to become?" The tools we offer boys today for managing their emotions will likely be the tools they will use one day if and when they are husbands and fathers. How many wives today wish their husbands had been allowed to feel and express their emotions as boys? Men and women have inherent differences, there's no question, but forcing boys to disconnect from their True Selves has only widened the gap.

*No one can make you feel inferior without your consent.*

– Eleanor Roosevelt

⌘

# 21

# When the Tears Are Fake

AS much as I stress the importance of honoring tears, it goes without saying that they are not always authentic. We all learn how to employ them at will as a form of manipulation from a very young age. Knowing this allows us to step back and analyze a situation before becoming overly influenced by the presence of tears. Babies depend on us to provide for their needs, so when babies cry, we have an obligation to react appropriately. But did you know that at the tender age of six months, babies become aware of cause and effect and, therefore, the power of crying to get your attention? They have been on this Earth for as little as 180 days and already they have figured out how to manipulate their caregivers with tears. Consider how much practice that means they may have had by the time they're in school. It certainly offers a new perspective on how we interpret tears.

There are times when we are certain we are dealing with crocodile tears. In those instances, speaking in an even tone, we can say, "How long do you plan on crying? I'm just wondering if I should stick around so we can talk about how the choice you are making is wrong. Otherwise, I can leave you alone for a bit and I'll come back when you're feeling calmer." That may sound callous, but it is kind to be firm. If we do not call children out on their manipulations, then we are simply reinforcing the behavior. Remember, I'm talking about the fake tantrum tears. The ones where you have witnessed the child get refused what he wants so he stomps off in an exaggerated rage, working himself up to get the tears to flow.

## Name What You See Without Accusation

It is not uncommon for children to cry at school. It would be fair to say that I assist at least a handful of students in tearful distress on a weekly basis. Considering the fact that I have been teaching for over fifteen years, you could say that I have seen a lot of tears in my career. I suppose this has helped me learn to decipher between true pain and manipulation with fairly good accuracy. Most of the time, however, especially if we are just getting to know the child, we need to do some investigating before we turn to our tough love techniques. This is what I refer to as "naming what we see without being accusatory". We don't judge the child's tearful reaction. Instead, we offer the child a clear explanation of why we are guiding them in a particular direction. The following tearful scenario took place a few years ago on the second day of third-grade. It involved a little girl who wanted to change her locker buddy.

Approaching me with a smile and a sweetness in her voice, she asked, "Miss Kathleen, can I please change locker partners?"

"I'm sure you remember the guidelines I gave yesterday, Taisha. I said that we need to be sure about our choice because once we choose our partner, we must honor that commitment for the school year. I only make changes if I feel it is truly necessary," I replied calmly.

"But when Jordana asked me to be her partner, I didn't know that Ophelia also wanted to be my partner, and I want to be Ophelia's partner, too. Please, Miss Kathleen, can we switch?", she begged.

Calm but unwavering, I replied, "Taisha, you and Jordana were two of the first students to choose to be together as partners yesterday. I clearly recall asking you both if you were sure, and you both happily answered, 'Yes!'. You had your chance yesterday to speak with Ophelia, but you didn't take it. The guidelines were clear. We won't be making any changes."

Bursting into tears, she exclaimed, "But I really want to be with Ophelia!"

This is where I had a choice to make. I could give in to her request, I could get angry at her exaggerated reaction, or I could seize the opportunity to try to reprogram her behavior. Personally, I found the latter of these three options to be the most appealing. There was no way I could set a precedent of changing my mind about guidelines on the second day of school. Doing so would make me lose all credibility. I was not interested in dealing with unreasonable, tearful outbursts all year long either. From my perspective, Taisha had presented me with an ideal chance to nip a problem in the bud. We teach people how to treat us. My goal was to establish, through kindness, that this behavior would not work with me.

I began by naming what I saw. "Taisha, I see that you are upset about not being allowed to change locker partners, and it's okay to cry if you need to, but you need to know that my mind's made up," I explained in an even tone.

Notice that I did not tell her that she should not be crying. In fact, I accepted her tears. Whatever we fight against is bound to put up resistance. By acknowledging her tears, I let her know that her reaction would not be the determining factor in the outcome of this exchange.

"It's not fair!", she continued.

"Actually, Taisha," I replied, keeping a calm, even tone, "what's not fair is you thinking that I ought to make an exception for you when the guidelines I gave everyone for choosing a locker buddy were quite clear. I explained from the beginning that everyone needed to reflect on their choice and be committed to that partnership for the long-term because I would not be making any changes."

It was honestly quite shocking to witness the force of her tears. The reaction seemed quite incongruous for her age and the issue at hand. I could not help but think that crying was a strategy that worked well for her at home. She had probably learned that if she cried long enough she would eventually get what she wanted. (This is a good example of what I mean by the inevitable need to sometimes make assumptions, without committing ourselves to them. They can be helpful in our attempts to find solutions to problems.)

Taisha and I were just beginning to build our relationship, and if there is one core principle I subscribe to as a parent, a teacher, and a friend, it is this: The person you are speaking to must perceive you as their ally. If you do not yet have a positive rapport with this person then not only do you risk being unsuccessful in finding a positive outcome to the scenario, but you also guarantee yourself an upward battle with that person the next time an issue arises (and chances are issues will arise often since that person will have very little intrinsic motivation to monitor her behaviors around you).

If Taisha is bluffing and trying to manipulate me, can I really blame her? Is it really the fault of an eight-year-old if she has learned that this behavior gets her what she wants? Rather than feeling frustrated by her tearful outburst, I felt compassion towards her. One of my obligations as a grade three generalist teacher is to assist children in communicating effectively. Teaching her how to react appropriately when she doesn't get what she wants is an ideal, real-life situation for evaluating this objective.

So rather than going the old-school route of "I'll show her who's boss!", I took a kinder approach. I delicately made a statement that could potentially call her bluff, if she was indeed bluffing. It is being honest without being hurtful.

"Taisha, I may be wrong, but I cannot help but think that you are used to getting what you want by crying. Here's what you need to know about me: I will always treat you fairly, and I will always be caring towards you, but I am not afraid of tears. They may get my attention, but when you are using them to trick me, they will have the opposite effect than what you may be hoping for. It's important that you learn that when

I have set out clear rules, I expect them to be followed. This experience has taught you to be more careful in following my instructions. I care very much about teaching you the right thing. Go and take a minute for yourself in the washroom to freshen up and come back to class ready to focus on the lesson."

That interaction with Taisha was a powerful one. She received the message that my kindness was rooted in teaching her the right thing. I have always found it interesting to hear parents' reactions when they happen to witness these type of interactions. It has happened on several occasions where parents have whispered to me afterwards, "I don't know how you do it. I would have just broken down and given them whatever they wanted. You are so strong." I'm not so sure that it's a question of strength, so much as a deliberate choice on my part to interpret the language of tears differently. We sometimes make the mistake of giving into tears, thinking that we are being kind, when in fact it is a true disservice to the child. Taisha learned very quickly that the "pity card" does not work with me. My response allowed her to develop more mature strategies when addressing her concerns with me. The smile on her face each day as she hugged me and said, "Good morning!", was all I needed to know that I had done her a huge favor by not encouraging her tears.

## Whining Is Much Like Tears

We almost always get to choose what we respond to, and how we respond to it. Let's take a simple example of a child who has a tendency to whine. Like anything else, this is a learned behavior that has been either reinforced or tolerated. Otherwise, she would not have this habit. Personally, I cannot stand whining (I really don't know how anyone does). Much like tears, a child will whine because it works. If you are a student in my class, however, it won't take you long to learn that it will never work with me.

The first whine from a child gets an answer such as, "Pardon me?", inciting her to try again. The second whine gets, "I don't understand you when you whine. When you are able to ask me nicely, I will respond to you." And when she does finally get it right, I am certain to reinforce her positive behavior by saying with a big smile on my face and authentic warmth in my voice, "There you go! I knew you knew how to speak kindly! See how nice it feels to ask for something in a polite way? Do you feel the difference in your body?"

Some kids will say my name over, and over, and over, and over again, thinking that they'll get my attention quicker. "Sweetheart," I'll interject, "The more you repeat my name, the slower I will be in giving you my attention. I will make you wait longer on purpose because you felt that you should get priority over all the others who have been patiently waiting their turn." It's a gentle dose of tough love. As with anything, when they do show me the expected behavior, they are congratulated for it with words of encouragement. I'll still make them wait a bit, but not too long. When training new behaviors, we need to be reasonable in our expectations. Statements such as, "Good job learning to be more patient," and "Thank you for understanding that there is only one of me and 26 of you," can go a long way in teaching kids that kindness makes the energy in the classroom so much more pleasant. We spend five days a week together, so let's make it enjoyable!

I am not saying that all transformations will happen overnight. In the case of Taisha, I noticed a clear improvement within the first couple of months of school. For some kids, however, it can take them until the last week of school. No matter how consistent you are in your strategies, each child learns and matures at their own rate. It can be hard to be patient, and you can forgive yourself when you do lose your patience, but be sure to ask for the child's forgiveness, as well.

## A Tip for Parents

Just as teachers use a new grade level as a means for encouraging maturity in children, birthdays are a perfect annual opportunity for parents to raise the bar. As children reach their annual milestone, we are provided with the chance to reflect and take stock of where they are developmentally. What behaviors should they be outgrowing at this point? What new responsibilities can be introduced? Though we should not force our kids to grow up too fast, we must not forget that they sometimes need a good nudge in the right direction to gain more independence. It's as simple as saying, "I don't know about you, but I don't like how things are going right now. It's time for a new approach. Let's come up with a plan that works for both of us."

*Have patience.*
*All things are difficult before they become easy.*

– Saadi

⌘

# 22

# Let's Replace Respect with Kindness

WHAT if we were to get into the habit of replacing the instruction, "be respectful" with, "be kind"? This simple switch could easily and naturally change the tone of a conversation altogether, and would most likely lead to more positive outcomes. When delivering a message with the word, "respect," it is easy to take on a tone of command or superiority, which is not always conducive to defusing a situation. On the flip side, try saying, "Be kind!!!!" in a bossy way. The results are quite ridiculous. I've tried. The use of "kind" in place of "respect" helps to teach a lesson by giving the child a clear action to take in order to solve a problem. It avoids the possibility of accusing a child of having poor character and instead empowers them by providing an opportunity to be seen as kind.

For example, in a school setting, instead of saying, "You just cut in front of Adriana in line. Show some respect," we could say, "Do you think it's kind to cut in front of someone? What *should* you have done?" Read those phrases aloud to yourself. Which one is easier to deliver in a kind voice? It's not impossible to say, "Show some respect," in a kind yet firm manner, but it requires more effort to keep your tone in check. Having said that, we must also resist using a judgmental tone when saying, "Do you think it's kind to behave that way?" Our tone of voice must be caring, otherwise the message of kindness will be lost.

In a family setting, instead of saying, "Your sister was talking and you just interrupted her. Show some respect," we could say, "Do you like it when your sister interrupts you? What would be the kind thing to do?"

Consider the above examples and ask yourself which of these phrases would you prefer to have spoken to you, given the choice? Can you feel the difference in energy and intention in each of these options? Though I have not conducted any kind of official survey, I have certainly seen the results from both forms of intervention. If the goal is to communicate to a child that she is being rude, without any concern for her feelings and without any real intention to teach her a better way of behaving, then the first intervention fits the bill. However, if the goal is to communicate to a child that her actions were impolite and to inspire her to replace her current action with a kinder one, then the second intervention becomes the obvious way to go. You see, both comments are legitimate, but the extra effort you make with the second comment is an investment in the child's well-being, as well as a gift of kindness and compassion. Keep in mind, too, that everyone in the vicinity, including yourself, gains from the second message, as all will feel the positive energy created by your words. Similarly, the first message affects everyone as well. Unfortunately, it tends to kill joyfulness.

## Pay Attention!

I'm not claiming that I never use phrases with a tone of harshness. I have heard them leave my mouth on more than one occasion. It's almost scary how naturally the words come out, too. After all, it's a language that was familiar to many of us as children, myself included. Phrases, such as, "Smarten up!", "Get it together!", "What's wrong with you?", "What were you thinking?", or "Pay attention!", were just a normal part of my upbringing. But I don't think any of us who has these childhood memories can claim that it felt good to be spoken to in this way. I'm not saying that we never "deserved it", but I am confident that this type of language does more harm than good, and I know for certain that better options exist.

## Catch Yourself

No one changes overnight, but by simply paying closer attention to your words before you speak, you can begin to notice the shift in energy that takes place in both yourself and the child with whom you are speaking. When you notice that your words have created pain, you can seize the opportunity to apologize for your words, to rephrase what you said, and to make a conscious mental note on how you plan to react the next time. In so doing, you will start to reprogram yourself.

The truth of the matter is that we all forget or slip up sometimes. The more I've learned to be kind to *myself* when I make a mistake, the more gentle I've become in how I communicate with children when they need to be "set straight". A twinkle in my eye and a softness in my voice goes a long way in helping a child to correct his behavior without making him feel bad about himself. This simple effort on the part of adults goes a long way in protecting children from exhibiting aggressive behaviors. I firmly believe that many kids are lashing out at others due to a lack of compassion in their lives. It is highly unlikely that a child who has a true sense of belonging could ever become the school bully. The less "respect" a child demonstrates to those around him, the more we must prove to him that he is worthy of our love and attention by modelling the behavior we wish to see.

The next time a harsh comment surfaces in your mind, try switching it out with one of these kinder reminders:

Instead of saying, "Pay attention!", why not give a gentle tap on the shoulder, signal with a little singsong, "Yoo-hoo!", or invite the child to get up and stretch.

Instead of saying, "Smarten up!" or "Get it together!" or "What's wrong with you?", try asking the child, "Are you alright?" or "Is something bothering you?" or "Can I help you with something?"

Instead of saying, "What were you thinking?", first consider how truly useless that question is…Clearly, to prompt that question, the child just did something thoughtless. It is obvious that he did not think first. He simply acted. A more constructive reaction on your part could be, "Do you see how that was not a good idea? Can I help you figure out how to keep from reacting that way next time?"

Experience has taught me that using the word "kind" instead of "respect," accomplishes at least two things. For one, it is difficult to argue with the word, "kind," as its definition is so clear. "Respect," on the other hand, can be vague and lead the child to challenge the statement by being defensive, "I was just borrowing it for a second! Big deal!" Remember that children, like adults, want to be seen as good. Accusatory statements can put people on the defensive and rarely is that ever helpful.

## The Only Thing I Am Judging Is The Act of Judging Itself

It can feel like demanding respect works. Usually, the act of saying the words makes us feel important and worthy. If anything, our words reassure us that we deserve respect. Listening to ourselves, we feel like we have made a strong, valid point. But if we fail to look into the eyes of our audience, we miss out on valuable information. The day I chose to truly look at the children receiving my instructions to, "Be respectful!", I realized they often looked confused, lost, or hurt. I have even unwittingly brought children to tears. It dawned on me that, often, kids have no idea what they've done wrong. When our frame of mind is focused on demanding respect, it can lead to wrong assumptions. Let's imagine the following interaction:

"Jonathan! What are you doing grabbing the ball out of Gabriel's hands?! That's so disrespectful!", I call out.

Jonathan responds, "But Miss Kathleen, it's my ball and Gabriel just stole it from me!"

False accusations are no fun, and now I'm stuck having to redirect my attention, which means that the impact of my intervention is no longer very credible.

In order to smooth things over, I'll probably say something like, "Gabriel, you can't just take things away from others. Jonathan, next time use your words, okay?"

When we are wrong (which often happens when we judge too soon), we rob children of the chance to solve problems their own way and the one who was already feeling upset or cheated may unwittingly end up feeling even worse.

Here's how that scenario could have gone differently if I had come from a place of kindness and helpfulness, instead of being judgmental and making assumptions.

Approaching the boys, I ask, "Is there a problem, boys?"

Jonathan responds, "Gabriel stole my ball from me, so I'm taking it back."

"Oh? Is that true, Gabriel?", I ask, looking him in the eye.

Notice that I address them by name. (If I don't know their names, I am sure to ask.) Using a child's name helps to build a connection and unconsciously establishes accountability.

Gabriel shrugs his shoulders and blurts out a quick, "Yeah. Sorry."

I could just let it go, but I love opportunities that highlight the importance of kindness, so I ask, "Was that kind of you, Gabriel?"

"Not really," he replies honestly.

"What would have been kind?" I prompt. Asking him to provide an example of kindness serves him in two ways. The act of thinking about it himself means he's more likely to take ownership of the idea and he is, therefore, more likely to remember to choose this route the next time he finds himself in a similar situation.

"I could have asked him if I could borrow it or if we could play together," he suggests.

Turning my attention back to the other child, I ask, "What do you think, Jonathan?"

"If he's going to share properly, he can come play with us," Jonathan replies.

Jonathan's willingness to cooperate stems from the fact that Gabriel offered the solution, rather than the teacher. If the solution had come from me, Jonathan may have played along, but a reticence would have been discernible. He would have been less convinced that Gabriel was truly going to cooperate.

When we filter our perception of events through the lens of kindness, we automatically have access to a whole new set of strategies and ideas. It's a non-confrontational approach that leads to happier and more constructive outcomes. At no point would Jonathan have felt that the teacher was wrongfully accusing him due to false assumptions. (You have surely noticed by now that I believe one of the most useful techniques to avoid making assumptions is to ask unbiased questions.)

I'm not saying that we stop teaching about respect. What I am suggesting is that we make kindness the first stepping stone on a child's journey to learning how to be respectful. Let's stop being indignant with children who seem to lack respect. Instead, let's give them the concrete tools for being respectful, which ultimately comes down to acts of kindness and empathy. Let's remember that their brains, their spirits, their hearts and souls are still developing...all the way through the primary years and beyond. Instead of condoning their mistakes, let's accompany them on their journey in a heartfelt way. By placing our attention first and foremost on kindness, we naturally teach respectful behavior.

Will there be exceptions to this rule? Of course. Exceptions are a part of life. Sadly, I can think of a few students from my past who resisted any kind of intervention from adults. For these troubled kids, I believe the interventions began too late. It became an uphill battle, and the lack of resources in the schools were in part to blame. It is for these children, especially, that I am writing this book. These are the kids who heard one too many times that they just didn't fit in. That they were not good enough. Or on the flip side, and equally damaging, they learned that the rules did not apply to them. They had not been taught empathy, compassion, or kindness in a concrete way. Their egos were out of control.

We can and should insist on particular behaviors that look and feel like respect. But demanding respect from children is pointless. Children are excellent judges of character. Be kind to them and they will be kind to you. We should not lose hope either if the kindness is not immediately returned from a child. We do not know the baggage they bring with them into our classrooms. Though we do not accept rudeness, we find the strength within ourselves to model patience. Authentic respect looks and feels like kindness.

Bottom line: ask yourself the following question, "When have you been the most motivated to do your best?" I am certain that when you felt valued you were willing to go above and beyond. Children are no different. In fact, what I love about kids is that they are less likely to "fake it" for anyone. Their honesty is worth a pound of gold when we honor them and challenge them authentically.

*It is better to light a candle than curse the darkness.*

– Eleanor Roosevelt

⌘

# 23

# Give Up the Control

TOO often I see adults swooping in to rescue children from conflicts. While I'm the first to say that we ought to nip problems in the bud, we also need to know when to let kids figure things out for themselves. By all means, we should discreetly monitor the situation, but we must resist intervening, as much as possible. Struggle is a natural condition of life. We may not enjoy the process of struggling but we need to understand that it is through this process that we grow. We must realize that when we intervene too soon and take control, we essentially rob children of the opportunity to gain experience and valuable life lessons.

Consider the transformation of a caterpillar into a butterfly. Without the struggle required to emerge from its cocoon, the caterpillar cannot complete its journey to becoming a butterfly. Its wings gain strength from pushing against the structure that was once its home and, in so doing, it gains the strength it needs to fly. If the butterfly is robbed of the chance to force its way out of its cocoon, it actually loses its ability to fly. We *disable* the butterfly, and it is unable to live its life as nature intended.

Think of when a child learns to crawl, pull himself up, walk and, eventually, run. Much like the caterpillar's transformation, the steps involved in learning to do to all of these things are accompanied by struggle. The child must work at it. The struggle serves a real purpose. Through trial and error, the required muscles gain strength and flexibility and, simultaneously, the brain makes neurological connections. It is nature's design.

If you are a parent, think back to how eager you were to see your child go through each of these steps. Yes, you guided him, held his hands, and basically encouraged him every step of the way. However, the real work was done by your child, not by you. This is the reference point I encourage you to use, and the frame of mind I want you to embrace, every time your child is faced with a problem. The growth that comes from struggling with an issue is comparable to the growth that comes from learning to walk. Learning to be mobile on his own is a necessary form of independence. So is learning how to deal with his personal problems, whether they involve his siblings, his peers or his teachers.

Let's consider a common interaction between siblings to see how we can foster independence in conflict resolution. I firmly believe that how our children deal with issues outside of the home begins with how we guide them within the home. When we insist on kindness between siblings, it inevitably spills over into the way they interact with the world at large.

For this scenario, we'll imagine that two sisters are playing together with their toys. The eldest is five years old and the youngest is two years of age. All is going fine when suddenly we hear the youngest sister, Lily, start to cry. Glancing over, it looks like the eldest sister, Beatrice, has taken a toy away from her little sister.

Here's what we should not do. Addressing the older child, the parent calls out, "Beatrice! Show some respect to your sister! You don't just grab the toy out of her hands." To which Beatrice replies, "But I had it first! She's always just taking my things. Argh!!". And Beatrice stomps off in a rage. A beautiful play session between siblings is ruined and a precedent is set for future conflicts to play out in much the same way, and that's a shame.

I'm sure we've all witnessed this common reaction from a parent, and we may be guilty of it ourselves. An interaction like this leads to frustration and does nothing to build the relationship between the girls. Not only is the parent taking away the opportunity for the girls to find a solution, but she is making an assumption instead of asking what just happened.

When we remind ourselves that, as parents, it is always our job to guide our kids to becoming the young adults we wish them to be, and that a problem is merely a situation looking for a solution, we can have a more productive and empathetic intervention.

Walking over to join the girls, the parent calmly explains, "Beatrice, if you don't find it kind when Lily grabs the toy from you, then you're being equally unkind towards her right now."

Beatrice replies (much like before), "But I had the toy first and she just took it from me, so I took it back!"

"Fair does not mean equal, Beatrice," the parent continues, "If Lily were to hit you with all her strength, would you hit her back with all *your* strength?"

"No, of course not, Mom!" she replies indignantly.

Guiding her towards making a connection, you ask, "Why not?"

"I'm a lot stronger and bigger than her. I could really hurt her," she answers logically.

"Exactly. But there are different kinds of hurt, aren't there? Lily is still learning that it's not nice to take things out of people's hands. But when she sees that her big sister does it too, the message gets confusing for her. How do you think you learned to share? You didn't have any siblings to share with while growing up. You learned it with me. Do you think I would grab toys out of your hands?"

Laughing at the thought, Beatrice responds, "That would be silly, Mommy! You're a grown-up!"

"You are the oldest child in this family, Lily. In many ways that is a privilege. Your sister will look up to you in a way that you will never completely understand. With this comes the responsibility to teach your sister the right way to do things. Treat her the way you want to be treated and she will learn, in time, to be just as kind to you as you are to her. Use your words, show her how to share properly, and if you need my help, just ask me."

The teaching of this kind of lesson needs to start young. You surely noticed as well that I substituted the word kindness for respect in the latter example. Once again, we see how a simple swapping of terms can set a completely different tone.

## My Child Is Not Mine

No person ever belongs to another. Be it from The Universe, God, or a fluke of nature, a child is merely on loan to us. We are entrusted by some greater force to care for a child, but the child is not ours. Viewing parenthood through this lens helps us to better see our role as a parent. The natural evolution of life is that the bird must leave its nest in order to make a nest of its own. Love comes in many forms. To allow our child to struggle is a form of love. Our words of encouragement and support carry them through their difficult times. Our belief in their abilities to find solutions builds their self-esteem.

If you are the type of parent who has allowed your child to fall and to get back up on his own, then you are already off to a good start. If you are the type of parent who has swooped in at the slightest trip or stumble, this may be more challenging for you. Think about how quickly the first years of your child's life have gone. There is no time to waste in helping your child learn to spread her wings. I invite you to calculate how many years you have left during which you can pretty much count on being the greatest influence in your child's life; before the teen years hit and you are faced with the dilemmas presented by peer pressure. Let's say your child is eight years old and that peer pressure begins around eleven years of age. That means you have about three good years left to help her build a decent base of confidence in her ability to take care of herself and to make smart decisions. Just three years before another child tries to convince her to think otherwise. Self-esteem is tightly linked to being confident in one's ability to act independently. Trial and error is the only way to develop these skills effectively. It is our duty as parents to equip our child with the necessary tools to navigate through daily life with enough self-confidence to ensure she stays on the right path when faced with difficult decisions. The experience she gets now will be her guide.

*(Children) must be allowed to have a childhood.*
*But they must also be allowed to find their courage*
*and their wisdom, and learn when to stand*
*and when to run away. After all,*
*if they are not permitted to climb the trees,*
*how will they ever see*
*the great and wonderful world*
*that lies before them?*

– Lian Tanner

⌘

# 24

# I Hate Math!

CHILDREN don't need to be in school for very long before they figure out their academic strengths and weaknesses. It's sad, really. I wish we would create a new system where report cards with letter grades and percentages were replaced with a continuum map for the individual child. We know that kids develop at their own rates, and yet the reporting system rates their degree of success not against themselves, but against an expected level of achievement. It's no wonder that each year I am faced with students who declare their weaknesses with conviction. It's heartbreaking to witness, but I love a good challenge, so when a student makes a statement such as, "I hate math!" or "I hate writing!", my response is pretty much the same. "No, you don't," I assure him, "You just haven't learned to love it yet." Of course, I realize not every child will learn to love math (or reading or writing or science) but I will certainly do everything in my power to get them to no longer cringe at the thought of it. I do my utmost to reprogram the voice in their heads. Being kind starts with our own self-talk.

One of my favorite ways to challenge a strong belief is by asking the student if he likes to eat. (I can relate just about anything to food.) The conversation goes something like this.

"Really? You hate math?", I'll say, tongue in cheek, "So you must not like chocolate chip cookies or your Grandmother's famous spaghetti sauce."

That catches a child's attention. The look in her eyes says something to the effect of, "What is this woman talking about?"

I'll continue, "Math is everywhere, especially when it comes to the food we eat. You need to be able to measure the ingredients to make something taste just right. You need to control the temperature of the oven and the length of the cooking time. There may be things you do not like about math, and we can work on that, but the only way I'll allow you to say that you hate math is if you also hate cookies." That always gets a smile out of the student. And where there is a smile, there is hope.

## I'll See It When I Believe It

I believe it is essential we make children think about what they are saying, and there is no better way to achieve this than by using examples of the things they love. Throw in a touch of humor, and "Voilà!" you've created a meaningful and memorable learning experience.

I've said it before and I will say it again, "Say what you mean and mean what you say, nicely." The language we use is the language not only those around us hear, but it's what we ourselves hear, as well. Of course, I follow up these little chats on a more serious note. "Each time we say to ourselves, 'I hate math', we succeed in reinforcing that idea," I tell them. "How can that possibly do us any good? It can't, which is why it is essential we be more honest and accurate about what we feel and why we feel it. To say you hate an entire language, since that's what math is, is far too drastic and dramatic.

"Instead, say to yourself, 'I find this challenging, but I am working at getting better.' Or, 'I may learn slowly, but once I focus long enough on a concept, I do eventually get it.' Or even, 'This is a subject which forces me to build my character and my patience with myself.' "

I do not allow my students to simply give up on an entire subject. I let them know that I do not expect them to be at the top of the class nor will I compare them to the top of the class. I will only ever compare them to themselves. When they hand in their work I will ask, "Is this *your* best?" Bit by bit, I will raise the bar higher, but it will always be within their reach. I tell them, "I realize you will not always believe in yourself as much as I believe in you, but that won't stop me from pushing you. I come from a place of love. I know what kids are capable of once they get out of their own way."

We need to be honest with our children about the reality of the school system if we expect to motivate them to do their best. That may sound counter-intuitive, but I promise you, it isn't. Most teachers are truly doing their best to teach the content of the course in an interactive, interesting manner, all the while respecting the requirements of the district's educational program. That is no small feat. Whenever I hear the words, "This is boring…", my creative juices start flowing, searching for a way to improve the enjoyment of the task. I am not always successful. Some tasks are simply boring. Not everything we do is going to be exciting. And we shouldn't want everything to be exciting, either. If it were, we would no longer be able to appreciate the excitement. Our enjoyment of life is dependent upon experiencing opposites. For instance, we cannot fully appreciate joyfulness without knowing what it is to be sad. The law of opposites applies to every aspect of our lives. The classroom is no exception. While boredom is an invitation for us to analyze the necessity of a task, it doesn't necessarily mean that we can simply do away with it. No matter what, my students need to learn their multiplication tables. But I can make it interesting. We can create games, we can sing them, we can dance them, and we will manage to enjoy ourselves, at least a bit. Boredom is the birthplace of creativity. It all comes down to the art of reframing the situation.

## Reading Can Be Boring

The love of reading is something we promote in school, and for good reason. Literacy skills open doors for us. My favorite success story took place a few years back with a boy named Ben. Not every student is passionate about reading, and this student in particular claimed he found it quite boring. It was painful to watch him during reading time. His usual, fun-loving disposition transformed into one of complete disinterest. He would do anything and everything other than connect with the books in front of him. It wasn't a question of decoding either. I knew he could read the words on the page.

My theory about Ben's lack of interest is one that applies to just about anything, really. He had not found the right reason to be interested, yet. And who can blame him? Our ability to understand oral language and visual media develops faster than our ability to understand the written word. It isn't hard to see why books have difficulty competing with the plethora of visual and audio media which flood the market these days. Growing up, we had cartoons on Saturday morning and we rented movies at the video store on Friday night, if we were lucky. Today's children have access to highly engaging visual-audio entertainment on a daily basis. These stories often captivate their imagination in ways that books cannot, *especially for children who are still learning to read.* We need to adapt our expectations and be more patient.

Ben was passionate about science and the universe. He would often interject interesting bits of information during class. His knowledge came from documentary films and Youtube videos. This is what sparked Ben's curiosity. *The books that would interest Ben were not at his reading level.* In order for a book to rival that of a movie, a child's reading skills need to develop quite a bit. This takes time. It was not Ben's fault that a great deal of effort still needed to go into learning the skills to decode words on a page and string them together to form meaning.

If I were to make the mistake of applying old-fashioned expectations to our current reality, then I may have been tempted to say to Ben things like, "Just try harder!" or "Do your work!" I may even have been to lead to believe that Ben is just lazy or a spoiled brat. Needless to say, all of the above accusations would have been nothing but harmful. When we come from that frame of mind, we communicate to children that we don't believe they are giving it their best, when in fact they may be giving it their all and they just don't know how to do better. What I needed to understand was that Ben didn't see the purpose or the importance of improving his reading skills. We must never assume that what seems obvious to us is obvious to the child. Coming from a place of "kindness first" means I needed to put myself in Ben's shoes.

The world Ben was growing up in had taught him that his curiosity for knowledge could be satisfied by other means. My response to this was simple. First, I needed to stop denying his feelings and stop trying to control the situation. Second, I needed to expose him to literature that rivalled visual media.

My heart-to-heart with Ben took place only a few weeks into the school year. It went something like this.

"Ben, I get the feeling that you really don't like reading," I stated in an understanding voice.

"All these books are boring," he explained.

"I can tell by the things you talk about in class that you love to learn about science and the universe. Do you not like the books we have in class on these topics?" I asked.

"I already know everything in these books," he replied.

I expected that answer. I continued, "That's what I thought you might say. It must be frustrating for you to have so much knowledge and be curious to learn more, but not be able to find your answers in the books that we have in class." I placed a handful of higher level books on his desk and I asked, "Do you think you might want to be able to read *these* books one day?"

Ben flipped through the pages. There was tons of information to accompany the captivating images on the page. "Yeah, that would be cool," he answered.

"Here's the thing, Ben. I understand that your brain is ahead of yourself. You already know more than a book that's at your reading level can offer you right now. But nothing in life comes for free. We need to work for the things we want. The more committed you are to your reading practice today, the sooner you will be ready to read these books. Does that feel like something worth working for?"

"I guess so, yeah," he said, a light coming to his eyes that was not there before.

I was getting through to him, but we weren't finished yet. There is a lot more to books than those two subjects. In order to find books that he could enjoy on the way to his ultimate goal, I also needed to inspire him to broaden his horizon.

"I have also noticed that you have a great sense of humor. We have some really funny books in the class. Have you tried reading any of those yet?", I asked.

"It's hard to find a book I like," he answered.

"Here's what we're going to do, Ben. I am going to help you find books that I think you might enjoy. You will have a pile of books on your desk every day during silent reading time. Your obligation is to read at least several pages of a book in order to give it a chance. If you don't like it, then you can put it to the side. You do not need to finish it. You just need to keep trying. I am really confident that you will find a book you'll like, but there's no rush," I told him.

His reaction was interesting. He said, "I've always thought you had to finish a book once you start it."

"Up until now, the books you have been given to learn to read have been quite short, right? But now you're getting older. The rules are changing. What matters most now, especially during your free reading time, is that you understand what you are reading and that you enjoy it. I want you to think of yourself as an explorer. You are in search of discovering what you like. Along the way, you will discover things you do not like. That's okay. It's all part of learning," I explained.

This talk with Ben changed everything. It wasn't long before Ben no longer needed my support to choose books. My choice to accept his reality and remove certain constraints, coupled with giving him a purpose, allowed Ben to feel free to explore books at his own leisure.

It was only a couple of months later when the significance of this conversation hit home for me. It was during portfolio night when Ben's father pulled me to the side. With a huge grin on his face, he said to me, "The most amazing thing happened last week. I passed by my son's room on my way to bed and noticed that the light was still on. My first thought was, 'Sneaky little bugger, he's still up playing!'", he laughed wholeheartedly and continued, "You can't imagine my surprise when I peeked in to catch him up to no good and, instead, I found him reading in his bed! He was so into it that he didn't even see me. I snuck away and left him to it. He has never picked up a book by himself before. Ever. Whatever it is that you said or did, I can't thank you enough."

I didn't do anything magical. I just let Ben be himself, all the while setting a standard of expectations that I knew he could agree to. I empathized with his situation, and it made all the difference.

*I never teach my pupils.*
*I only attempt to provide the conditions*
*in which they can learn.*

– Albert Einstein

⌘

# 25

# Embrace Personality, Change Habits

WHEN it comes to teaching children how to improve themselves, it is important we show them the difference between their habits and their personalities. Children should never be led to believe that there is something intrinsically wrong with them. For instance, it can be part of a child's personality to feel uncomfortable in accepting a compliment, but it is a bad habit if, in order to deflect the attention, she responds by putting herself down. Likewise, it can be part of a child's personality to be competitive, but it is a bad habit to gloat about his accomplishments. Personality traits are aspects of a person that we must accept. It is only the habits associated with these traits that ought to be addressed. We have a responsibility to teach children to communicate kindly, not just with others, but as in the case of receiving compliments, with themselves, as well.

What fascinates me most about bad habits is that children are usually completely unaware of their behavior. Which, when you really think about it, explains a lot as to how a confrontation can emerge without the child ever understanding what he did wrong. I've seen it time and time again. A child unconsciously rolls her eyes at something someone has just said and the next thing you know, people are calling her rude or mean. We are so used to making assumptions about people's facial expressions and body language, and yet, how often are we wrong? Children mirror the world around them, which means they are often mindlessly mimicking behaviors. To what extent are they really the ones responsible for their behavior?

## When Bad Habits Affect Friendships

Each new class group may be a fresh start for the teacher, but we must not forget that the further along children are in their years at school, the more history these children already have with one another. Some of them may have even been at the same preschool or daycare prior to Kindergarten, giving them that much more time to have fixed impressions of their peers. The teacher who fails to acknowledge the pre-existing social dynamic in her classroom misses out on an opportunity to better comprehend conflicts and behavior issues when they arise. Let's take a common problem that occurs each September. A child will be nervous or reticent about coming into the classroom. When asked about it, two of the most common responses are, "I have no friends in this class," or "I'm not very good at school/I'm not smart." We already explored strategies for the latter of these two examples in the previous chapter. Now we will focus on the friendship comment.

Let's take Chelsea as an example. From the moment I set eyes on Chelsea, she seemed so tough and withdrawn, I wondered if I would ever be able to get through to her. One of my main goals as a teacher is to establish a positive connection with each and every one of my students, but some cases are always more daunting than others. I felt immediate concern towards Chelsea and I knew I would have to make a conscious effort to connect with her. It didn't take me too long to figure out that, like most kids with tough exteriors, she was actually a highly sensitive child. She had the bad luck of having been separated from her best friend for the new school year and she felt lost in the unfamiliar social dynamic. (By the way, this should never happen. I am a firm believer that when making class groupings, teachers ought to make sure that every child has at least one close friend for the new school year.)

As a result of whatever experiences Chelsea had already lived, she had developed a self-preservation shield that she believed protected her from being rejected. I do not believe she realized on a conscious level that this is what she had done, but when she confided in me that she felt lonely in class and that this was why she was not very motivated to do her work or to arrive to school on time, she gave me the opportunity to address some of her deflective habits that I had come to notice.

"It's no fun when it's time to pick partners and nobody comes to ask me," Chelsea told me one recess when it was just the two of us left in the hallway.

"Have you tried asking someone to be your partner instead of waiting for them to find you?" I asked in a calm voice.

"Sometimes, but usually they tell me they already planned to be with someone else. I just feel like they're avoiding me," she explained.

I'm going to suggest that a common adult response would be to say, "Why would you say that? Of course they're not avoiding you!" I understand the temptation to sooth the child's pain and to want to reassure them that everything is okay. But it doesn't solve the problem. It merely sweeps it under the rug. An observant teacher will have already noticed that kids are not approaching Chelsea to be their partner and/or that Chelsea holes herself up at her desk, casting an invisible shield around herself that effectively communicates to her peers that she is not to be approached. My response to Chelsea needed be honest. By the way, it takes courage to knowingly make someone uncomfortable with the truth. I did not find it the least bit easy to be saying something that I knew could cause Chelsea pain, but I had to trust that it was essential that Chelsea take ownership of the role she was playing in the problem, if she were to ever find a solution. I had to trust that, since I know it is kind to be authentic, I had the skills to guide the conversation in the right direction. Chelsea was asking for help, not for false reassurances.

Using the art of questioning, I carefully suggested, "What if they *are* avoiding you? Can you think of any reasons why someone might not be sure that they want to be your partner?" Chelsea needed to see herself through the eyes of others. In no way was I looking to make Chelsea feel badly about herself. Everything, from my gentle, understanding tone of voice -- to my relaxed posture, was designed to inform Chelsea that I cared for her and that I wanted to help.

I had caught Chelsea off-guard. She looked me in the eye, confused by the unusual question. "Are you saying it's my fault?" she inquired, slightly hurt.

"It's not about it being your fault. There is no need for blame or feeling badly. Whenever we are having trouble with something, and we realize we are experiencing this problem with a variety of people, not just one person in particular, it's a chance to ask ourselves if we are the ones who need to make a change. We can never control how people will react to us, but we can control how we react to others. I see how sweet and sensitive you truly are, but I think right now you are hiding it from the others," I explained.

"You think I'm sweet?" she interjected, with a tone of disbelief, but a sparkle in her eye.

"You are definitely a sweet girl, Chelsea! You can't hide from me," I replied. "Can we try something?"

"Sure," she agreed.

"I'm going to roll my eyes at you and I want you to tell me if it makes you feel anything, okay?", I explained.

"O...K..." she replied with a hint of sarcasm in her voice.

I rolled my eyes, mimicking her as best as I could, but with a hint of humor so that she knew I was not mocking her. She laughed and I joined in on the laughter. I then asked her, "I know I was being a bit silly, but how did it feel for me to roll my eyes at you?"

"It felt weird, I guess," she said.

"It certainly didn't feel good, right? What if that's what others are feeling when you roll your eyes in their direction? What do you think eye-rolling is meant to communicate to someone?", I asked, pushing her to make connections between her behavior and her current reality.

"I don't know...Maybe that you don't really care about what the person is saying?" she offered.

"Do you recognize yourself in that?", I continued.

"I know I roll my eyes sometimes, but I don't think it's that bad," she replied.

"Chelsea, what if I told you that you roll eyes *a lot*? I think you are just so used to doing it that you are not even aware. And what if I told you that this action is making the others in the class feel like they can't trust you? Would you want to work with someone who you knew might make you feel like they don't care about what you have to say?", I gently inquired.

"Is it really that bad? I'm not trying to be mean...It's just sometimes people ramble on or repeat themselves. It's annoying," she said.

"I'm afraid it is pretty bad, Chelsea. You know, you have a right to disagree with others and even to find what they say to be annoying, but most of the time, it serves us best to keep those opinions to ourselves, especially if we want to have a sense of belonging to the group. I have an idea that could help. What if each time I catch you rolling your eyes, I send you a secret signal for you to catch yourself and break the habit?", I suggested.

Chelsea liked the idea very much. And that was just the tip of the iceberg. Once she realized that she could be an active participant in changing how the others saw her, she began going out of her way to express her opinions in a constructive way. It was as if she had not realized that it was okay to disagree openly but constructively with others. She would catch herself "mid eye-roll" and quietly whisper, "Whoops, sorry," smiling kindly instead. It was a beautiful transformation. With time, others came to trust her and she built friendships in the classroom. We had many more productive conversations after that which led to even greater success for Chelsea in the classroom. The hundred-dollar question however is this: what happens next year if her teacher does not have the same approach or the same philosophy? Will all that hard work evaporate? Will it have been for nothing?

We need to expect that Chelsea may enter a new classroom with her old habits. Everyone can relate to falling into old patterns of behavior. Anyone who has made a resolution to quit smoking, to stop overeating, or to exercise more regularly ought to be able to see themselves in Chelsea's (possible) regression. I have heard adults scoff at these types of regressions by making statements such as, "See, she hasn't changed at all," and, "That kid has got a mean streak in her." I wish teachers could see how they create their own realities. It is common knowledge that 80% of communication is body language. If the thought you hold in your mind about a child is that they are mean, that child will feel that thought through your body language. How can we ever expect to gain a child's trust or build a relationship with her if she senses that you do not like her? Nobody enjoys the feeling of rejection, especially when it is from someone whom you wish you could look up to. Children should not be expected to be any different from adults, or at the very least, the bar should not be set higher for them than it is for us.

If you hold a negative opinion of a child's behavior, then figure out how to separate the behavior from the person. Do not assume or imply that this negative behavior, be it name-calling, rude remarks, or eye-rolling, is a true indicator of the person's character. Consider that this behavior is nothing more than a bad habit. Find the goodness in the child. Assume that this bad habit is masking an insecurity and find strategies to help them replace their bad habits with better ones. Find good, positive things to believe about the child and nourish those thoughts in your mind. This way, when you catch her doing the wrong thing, it will be easier for you to address the behavior empathetically. Refer to the behavior as a bad habit and coach her to replace that particular action with something more constructive. Adults rarely manage to quit smoking, to cut back on sweets, or to keep their gym commitment without using some kind of replacement strategy. Smoking can be replaced with chewing gum, sweets can be replaced with fresh fruit, and a gym commitment might stick when we check in with ourselves each day and realize how our energy is clearer and more positive after exercising. Empathy is identifying our own weaknesses and realizing we are not so different from one another after all. Children act as mirrors. They are not just pulling their behaviors out of thin air.

One more thought. Some of you may have noticed that I allow children to pick their partners rather than assigning them myself. It is only one of many ways that I set up partner work. I use a variety of strategies throughout the school year to pair or group children. It may be at random, or based on strengths, or based on interests. However, at the start of a new school year, I find I learn a lot about the social dynamic of my classroom when I allow the students to choose their partners. I then use these observations to foster healthy relationships.

*First we form habits, then they form us.*
*Conquer your bad habits or they will conquer you.*

– Dr. Rob Gilbert

⌘

# 26

# Is It Really a Bad Day?

FOR years now, I have been telling children that there is no such thing as having a "bad" day. Unpleasant things happen to all of us, and sometimes a series of unhappy events occur all at once, but all of it is temporary. The notion of having a "bad" day does not serve us. It is the opposite of being kind to oneself and it prevents us from being grateful for all that is good. The words we speak shape our reality. Why would we ever choose to have a "bad" day? You may say that it is not a choice. You may say it is a result of factors outside of our control. I'd like to suggest that the phrase, "I'm having a bad day," is a judgment, not an observation. What if, instead of saying, "I'm having a bad day," we were to say, "A bunch of unfortunate things have happened so far today." The latter of the two statements allows us to detach ourselves from the events that have taken place. The shift in focus keeps us from taking the events of the day personally. "I'm having a bad day" is the equivalent of casting a curse upon yourself. Watch your thoughts. They are powerful. If this is a phrase you are accustomed to using, then you should ask yourself, "Why?" Is it to indulge in self-pity or to seek out sympathy? Is it to give yourself permission to be grumpy and short-tempered for an *entire* day?

My feeling is that a whole day is quite a long time to be feeling bad, and life is much too short to commit ourselves to that state of mind for an entire day. I am not saying we never have bad days. Sometimes, no matter how hard we try to manage our thoughts, we can feel stuck in a rut. I still maintain that rather than saying, "I'm having a bad day," we ought to say, "I feel stuck. I'm looking for a way out of this." The second option is an invitation for finding a solution. It's a much more useful thought.

In order to teach children how to let go of this idea, we need to walk them through the thinking process. When I hear a child declare, "I'm having a terrible day!", my response is something to the effect of, "Oh no," showing genuine concern, "What happened?"

The child will then tell me whatever it is that is upsetting him. It may be just one thing, or it may be an unfortunate series of events. My first priority is to simply listen. I let him complete his list, and then I reply, "Are any of these things still happening right now?"

Typically, the answer is no. When this is the case, I continue by saying, "I'm sorry that these things have happened to you today. But like you just said, none of these things are still happening now. They can't be undone, but it's over. Do you agree?"

"I guess so," the child will say hesitantly.

"I'm going to let you in on a little secret that many adults don't even know. Ready?" (I say it like this because it makes a child feel important when they think they may know something that a grown-up doesn't. It also means I am more likely to make a lasting impression.) After a slight pause to ensure I have his attention, I explain, "You are free to change how you feel about your day at any given moment. There is no rule that says your whole day has to be bad just because that is how it feels right now. You might believe it to be true, but that is probably because we see other people acting that way. Just because some people believe in having a bad day does not mean you need to agree with them. I promise you that it feels wonderful to let go of your anger or sadness. It's a feeling of release. You will feel lighter when you choose to say to yourself, 'There is nothing I can do about what went wrong so far today, but I can look for good things to happen as of right now.'"

Time and time again I have witnessed children's emotional states transform before my eyes as they internalize this new way of seeing things.

"What would feel good right now?", I then ask the child. This gives them a concrete action to focus on. Much of what I have said so far is somewhat abstract. While I believe children are capable of understanding so much more than we typically give them credit for, we need to make sure they forge a link between theory and reality by helping them to live the experience. For instance, the child may suggest, "I could ask Sam if he wants to play with me," or "I think I'd feel better if I could write about it in my journal." As always, I use the art of questioning to prompt these ideas from the child. This helps him realize that he is capable of finding solutions on his own. Throughout the entire process, the child must be held in a state of engagement. He is being asked to think, to reflect, to choose, and to act.

The lesson doesn't finish here. To help solidify the message, I will check in with the child later on that day and ask, "How are you feeling now?" More often than not, the child will reply, "Good," and offer me a smile.

I then make sure I reinforce the work he did by saying, "I hope you are proud of yourself, because I sure am proud of you. You did really good work taking care of yourself today." I'll go on to say, "Do you notice how the energy in your body is different from before? Which feels better?" The goal here is to draw a child's attention to how their physical state is closely tied to their mental state.

## What if It Really Is a Bad Day?

Sometimes, though, life can throw some terrible things at us. Sometimes, we don't only feel like we're having a bad day...it feels like a bad week...even a bad year. That's all the more reason for us to take care of our internal dialogue.

What do we say to a student who tells us that they are going through something truly awful, like the death of a family member? This brings us back to the philosophy I mentioned in an earlier chapter. It is one of the reasons I tell my students repeatedly throughout the year that the classroom is a place where we can leave our troubles at the door. Nothing obliges us to carry our painful stories with us all day long. We can imagine the classroom as a bubble separate from our home lives. This can be so liberating for a child. My students always know that they are not obliged to tell me what is bothering them. They are entitled to their privacy.

In the previous script, I ask the child to explain why they feel they are having a bad day. The child who does not want to talk about it is going to simply stand there and look at you, or, even more telling, he will stare at the floor. When this happens, I let a little time go by, and if they still do not speak, I am sure to offer them a way out. I'll say, "Maybe you don't want to talk about it. That's okay. Let me just ask you one thing. Is the problem happening here at school or is it something outside of school?"

If the child says it's at school, then I will continue prompting him to share. It's something that I have an obligation to try to help him resolve. But sometimes the words are too hard to speak or even to find. When this happens, I will suggest he draw or write about it. This strategy tends to work really well. Once he's finished recording the problem, I will have him share it with me and we will look for solutions. I let him know that I may not be able to fix the problem immediately, but he should be proud of himself for bringing the issue to my attention.

But if the child says it is something that is happening outside of school, my course of action is different. I will say, "If it's something that is making you feel unsafe, I want you to know you can trust me. But if it's something personal that you just don't want to talk about, that's okay, you don't need to tell me. Remember, you can let the classroom be your bubble. When you catch yourself thinking about something that is making you feel upset, you can remind yourself that it is not happening right now, in this present moment, and you can try to let it go. Sometimes that's not easy, and you may want a few minutes outside of the classroom to take a walk around the school or to get some water. That's perfectly fine. You can just tell me you'd like a break and I'll let you go, okay?" Children feel relieved knowing that they have a safe "out" from the classroom. I know, as teachers, it can be hard to let our students leave the class when they ought to be working, but the urge to say they need to stay in class is counterintuitive. We need to realize that they need the break in order to regain their ability to concentrate. They will be more productive once they have had the chance to clear their minds.

It isn't always necessary to discuss our issues. Sometimes the best remedy is to take five minutes alone to breathe, to focus on the air flowing in and out of our lungs. Another great strategy is to take a moment to identify five things for which we are grateful in order to recenter ourselves and to move out of Ego and back to our spirit, our True Self.

There are times when we need to seek out compassion or support from our friends, but there are better ways to ask for this help than by claiming, "I'm having a bad day." Let's delete this phrase from our vocabulary. The next time we are feeling down or irritable let's try saying, "I'm having a bad *moment,*" or, "I'm not feeling very good right now." There's nothing wrong with talking about our problems. In fact, it can be very healthy. But I would argue that how we talk about our problems makes all the difference in the degree and duration of our suffering. How we frame our problems sets a tone for how others will respond to us, and more importantly, how we ourselves perceive our problems.

As we learn to change how we verbalize our feelings, we can't help but realize the harm we do when we label someone else's day as being bad. It's like casting a curse. We've all heard ourselves say to someone, "Are you having a bad day?" It's really not a helpful statement. Let's switch that line of thinking to, "Are you okay?", or "Do you need help with something?" Let's lead with questions that can bring us to a happier place.

## What Defines a Bad Day?

On a final note, I want you to take a minute to consider the various thoughts you've had throughout your day so far. How many of them were judgmental? For instance, did someone irritate you today by not holding the door open for you or by cutting in front of you in traffic? It can be tempting to feel indignant towards such thoughtless actions. But here's the thing. The literal definition of thoughtless is "without thought". The person was not thinking. Doesn't that happen to all of us? Is it really necessary to be harsh in our reaction? How we react in a situation is almost always a choice. It's okay to be upset in the moment. After all, someone's thoughtless action threw you for a loop. However, you get to choose how long you hold on to that emotion. Will the emotional charge disappear after a few moments, a few hours, or will it stay with you for the rest of the day? Will you still be thinking about it when you go to bed?

Chances are that the person who caused your suffering or feeling of indignation is completely oblivious to your pain; which means the only person responsible for your suffering right now is *you*. Judgmental thoughts rarely serve anyone. Consider the following synonyms for "judgmental": critical, fault-finding, condemnatory, disapproving, disparaging, deprecating, negative, overcritical, hypercritical, scathing. We can and should make observations about the world we live in, but as much as possible we must find ways to protect and maintain our inner peace. We can achieve this through empathy.

It bears mentioning that some of us seem to enjoy being judgmental. For some, there is an emotional high that comes from making oneself feel superior to another. It feeds the Ego. Being kind and forgiving can be boring. It feels good to be kind, but the high is not the same. This is another reason why I teach children to pay attention to their energy. I want them to realize that positive energy serves them better than negative energy. I want them to grow into adults who do not have these habits of making themselves feel better by putting others down.

I am sure, at one time or another, we all have judgmental reactions that make us feel superior. When I catch myself feeling annoyed towards someone, and I am saying to myself, "I would never have done that!", I immediately challenge myself to choose a new reaction by inventing a compassionate story. Let's say I'm entering a pharmacy and I am directly behind a lady who, rather than holding the door for me to catch it, simply allows it to close behind her. My initial thought might be, "How rude!" Upon realizing my lack of compassion, I choose to continue my thought process. It may go something like this, "She may not have held the door open for me because she did not realize I was behind her. She may not have thought to check because she is caught up in her mind about something. Maybe her child is sick and she has been up all night worrying. That could explain why she needed to come to the pharmacy. I can certainly forgive her for being oblivious to those around her." The goal is to arrive at the desired destination, i.e. acceptance and forgiveness. Could you really allow yourself to stay upset at a woman who is so consumed with worry for her child that she did not think to check if someone was behind her when she entered the store? This is an exercise in compassion and empathy that I practice regularly. Let's be honest. Plenty of people are caught up in their minds all the time, so we have ample opportunities to hone our skills. We also get to choose who to feed: the Ego or The Self. I contend that life is much more joyful when we nourish The Self. There is no better time to be kind and compassionate to ourselves, and others, than when we are feeling down.

## Two Wolves

An old Cherokee told his grandson,
"My son, there is a battle between two wolves inside us all. One is
Evil. It is anger, jealousy, greed, resentment, inferiority, lies,
and ego.
The other is Good.
It is joy, peace, love, hope, humility, kindness, and truth."
The boy thought about it, and asked,
"Grandfather, which wolf wins?"
The old man quietly replied,
"The one you feed."

— Cherokee legend

Author's Note: There are countless versions of this parable. This particular one is my favorite.

⌘

# 27

# Love Thy Enemy

AS much as I stressed in the previous chapter that we must stay away from the idea of a "bad" day, how do we address a problem that is ongoing? I have been asked on more than one occasion, "Kathleen, how am I supposed to be loving towards someone who is making my child miserable? She's crying every morning that she doesn't want to go to school. I am furious that this is going on and nobody is doing anything to stop it." It can be very challenging to see our child in tears and not wanting to go to school. There is a feeling of helplessness in knowing that the problem is occurring in a place that ought to be a safe haven for children. The first thing to keep in mind is that our reaction will influence the outcome. We must ask ourselves what we want our child to learn from this in order to guide us appropriately. Personally, I want children to see the world as a giant classroom. I also want children to believe that we are only given in life what we are strong enough to handle. These two beliefs help me to remember that I mustn't get over-involved, that is, I should not swoop in to save the day. We must teach children how to solve their problems with as much independence as possible. We should only intervene when it seems absolutely necessary. "To love thy enemy" means we have an obligation to empathize with the child who is causing our own child pain. Every conflict in our life is an opportunity to grow.

First, help your child to see that nothing is personal and that she does not need to see herself as a victim. I tell children that everyone comes into our lives for a reason and we must be ready to learn the lesson they are teaching us. I'll say, "Wow! The world better get ready for you! You are being taught such a huge lesson in self-love and forgiveness at such a young age! I cannot wait to see what you are being prepared for!" Do not make the mistake of thinking young children can't grasp these lessons.

The next thing is to resist jumping to conclusions. Our child may be crying every morning before school, but we must not assume that the teacher is aware of the problem. Our child may be telling us that the teacher is aware of what is going on, but we have to remember that a child's perception of events can differ greatly from that of the teacher. We must realize that we only established that the problem was ongoing when the problem actually reoccurred several times. The first morning our child cried was an isolated incident to us. The second time, we started to ask ourselves questions, but we still weren't overly concerned. The third time, it started to send up some red flags. And so on and so forth. A pattern had to emerge before we could realize that this was more than just a random upset between two kids. In the same vein that it took us some time to recognize that the problem was more serious than we first thought, we must allocate this time to the teacher, as well. As parents, we get more personal one-on-one time with our child than the teacher will ever have. Keep all of this in mind once you decide to contact the teacher.

When you do contact the teacher, you must resist being accusatory. Simply ask the teacher if she has noticed anything strange going on between your child and the one with whom she is having a problem. You can say you are worried and that your child has been crying and that you are looking for any information that she can offer you to shed some light on the situation. Leave out the word "bully" for now, please. You have only just learned of this problem. No one deserves to be labeled a bully if they have not yet had a chance to change their behavior. Furthermore, I must insist that we resist calling young kids "bullies", no matter what. Our words have the power to create labels, and labels are hard to shake. Once a child hears a label being attributed to him, he is likely to believe it and live up to it. We must pay attention to the messages children receive about who they are.

I have been witness to parents and teachers arguing about who did what to who. It makes me cringe. What kind of example is that? All adults must learn how to talk to one another about children's conflicts in non-confrontational ways. It can help if we reframe the incident. Let's realize that what we are talking about is how to teach children how to treat each other better. They are influenced by everything they see and hear around them. The less we over-react, the more peacefully we can resolve the issue, and the greater the lesson becomes for the children involved.

When the drive to protect our child begins to cloud our judgment, it helps to remember that no one ever said life is supposed to be easy. In the words of Brené Brown, "You are imperfect, you are wired for struggle, but you are worthy of love and belonging".

## There Are Three Sides to Every Story

Through the use of questions, engage your child in a conversation in order to better understand what is actually going on. There are *three* sides to every story: mine, yours, and the truth. We must remain open-minded and listen as much as possible to our child's perception of the problem. We have to clear our mind of judgments and assumptions or else we risk turning something that may be minor into something unnecessarily major. Some effective guiding questions are:

How do you feel when she calls you names (or pushes you)?

Why do you think you feel this way?

Does a part of you feel you deserve to be treated this way and that's what really hurts?

Is she right? Do you believe you are (stupid, dumb, ugly)?

Would you ever act that way towards someone else?

Why not (or why, if the case may be)?

What do you think makes someone act this way?

Do you think that someone who feels good about themselves would talk this way?

Does this person look happy to you?

This last question should be asked each and every time we discuss negative behaviors. Someone who is sincerely happy and at peace with life is not likely to be repeatedly hurtful or mean to someone else.

Explain to your child that there is only one person we can control and that is ourself. We must be loving and kind to ourselves. When someone says something hurtful to you, the talk in your head should sound something like this: *I know I am a good person and nobody deserves to be treated this way, including me.* And once your child gets good at thinking this way, encourage her to go the extra mile and say it out loud to her perceived victimizer.

## The Victim Must Take Control of the Situation

A child does not act hurtfully towards another child for no reason. There is always something at the root of their behavior. For one reason or another, that child is feeling unhappy and is taking it out on others. That *does not excuse* the behavior, but by understanding it, we can feel empathy and be motivated to reach out in a supportive way. Punishment and retaliation would only serve to confirm the child's belief that life is unfair and unkind. Taking the high road and reaching out to help the child shows her that even if life is a struggle, there is plenty of love to go around.

I had the opportunity to volunteer in my child's classroom and witnessed an interaction between Yasmine and her "victimizer". It was clear that Yasmine needed to change her reaction if she wished to separate herself from the problem. She was trying to "fix" the child's behavior by telling her what she was doing wrong. I'm sure I don't have to tell you how that played out. No one wants to be told what they are doing wrong, and this little girl, who was already being mean and controlling, would lash out at Yasmine. Of course, Yasmine felt hurt because she was only trying to help. What Yasmine needed help seeing was that she was not going to be able to help this little girl. Her problem was bigger than she could realize. It is four years later and now these two girls get along quite nicely at school. Yasmine's intimidator had personal issues with which she was struggling. Once Yasmine was able to see that the other child's behavior had nothing to do with her, she was able to separate herself from the pain this girl had been sending her way. She learned to say, "I like you, but I don't like it when you treat me this way."

Once again, it was the power of questioning which worked like a charm to get Yasmine to see this little girl's actions with compassion and forgiveness. I used the information she had shared in our daily conversations to help her make connections. Some of the questions were:

"Didn't you tell me she complains about her older sister being mean to her?" This helped her to see not only who was modelling the hurtful behavior, but also why it might seem normal to her.

"Didn't you tell me her parents just separated?" This helped her to see that this little girl was going through emotional turmoil.

"Didn't I hear you saying that she gets away with everything at home?" This helped her to see that she was begging to be given limits.

These types of conversations have permitted my children to detach themselves from the hurtful gestures of others. They have learned to not give their energy away by reacting negatively. In so doing, they avoid fueling the fire and they protect themselves from future conflicts. They know that they can either remove themselves from the situation or they can respond by saying something like, "I'll play with you when you're ready to be nice." An unhappy child who is hurting another child has chosen her target for a reason. There is something in the way the victim is reacting that is serving the victimizer.

## We Must Learn to Forgive Ourselves

"Why would the victim need to forgive herself?", you ask. Simple. Because there is no victimizer without a victim. Don't worry, I am not blaming the victim. In fact, I am not blaming anyone. We must forgive ourselves for believing the words that are spoken about us. We are born with a natural desire to belong, which means that every kind word spoken to us is internalized and categorized. We want to believe the good things that are said about us. But it starts to get confusing when others say things about us that are less than kind. What do we do then? We've been trained to believe what is said about us.

We must teach our child to recognize the role she is playing that encourages whatever is being said or done to her. She may or may not be in part to blame for what is going on. Be willing to accept that your child may be at fault here, too. Do not underestimate a child's desire to avoid getting herself in trouble by bending the truth to suit her needs. You were a kid once, so I know you know what I am talking about. Part of the solution to the problem may be that your child needs to apologize for something she did that led up to the event in the first place. We must teach our child to let go of her pride. Embarrassment is uncomfortable but it's a temporary state whose end result is a feeling of liberation. Our vulnerability makes us beautiful and loveable. Asking for forgiveness is humbling and at the same time empowering.

By the way, if you have no idea what goes on at school or have no sense of who your child spends time with at school, I strongly suggest you do whatever you can to get involved. If you cannot volunteer in class, then at least be sure to sit together for family discussions and let your child lead the conversation. In order for our kids to talk to us, we must create opportunities daily. In several of his books, Larry Winget points out that research shows parents, on average, are spending three and half minutes per week in meaningful conversation with their children. I agree with him wholeheartedly when he says that this information should make us feel sick. Is it any wonder that children need guidance in communicating appropriately with their teachers and their peers? Chances are you do not fall into this category of parents if you are reading this book. However, by realizing that your child's peers may be living this reality, it allows you to foster that much more empathy and compassion in your own child towards the challenges her friends may be facing.

I am not saying that it will always be this easy. What I *am* saying is that, more often than not, the problem is not as big as we make it. When we remind ourselves that we can choose to not be a victim, and we can choose to see the victimizer through compassionate eyes, we not only contain the problem and minimize the pain, but we also offer a gift of love to both ourselves and our aggressor.

*When another person makes you suffer,*
*it is because he suffers deeply within himself,*
*and his suffering is spilling over.*
*He does not need punishment; he needs help.*

– Thich Nhat Hanh

⌘

# 28

# The Friendless Child

NOT everyone has an easy time making friends. Some children are socially awkward and, in spite of their best efforts, have difficulty being accepted by the group. There are various reasons for this. For some, it may be due to a lack of maturity, for others, they may need to be explicitly taught the necessary skills. These children may have disabilities, which may or may not be diagnosed. While I am the first to say that we cannot force friendships, every child deserves to feel appreciated and included, one way or another. I have a particular approach I like to use to help foster healthy relationships for these children.

It's usually quite obvious when a child is having trouble bonding with others, but it can take time before a teacher can effectively address the situation. Signs of exclusion or teasing will surely show themselves in the classroom but, mostly, it takes place on the playground, where it is harder to be seen by the adults. Moreover, it is not usually just the child's classmates with whom he'll experience difficulties, making the situation that much more complex.

It may take a month or two together as a class before I feel our connection is strong enough to broach the subject. I need to be sure that I have assessed the situation accurately. I also need to make sure I have plenty of qualities to point out about the child and I interject them throughout the conversation when need be. For this example, I will name this boy, Cadden.

Typically, for my intervention to be effective, something major needs to occur. Often what will happen is the 'Caddens' of our world will explode in frustration. His classmates will witness this explosion and no one will know quite what to do. This is usually an opportune time to launch my intervention. Cadden's emotional outburst provides concrete proof to his classmates that he is suffering.

I arrange for Cadden to leave the class, I close the door, I turn off the lights, and in a low voice, I begin, "Boys and girls, I need your attention. Please stop what you are doing right away. I don't mean to interrupt you, but this is serious. I need to talk to you about something very important and I may not have very much time." I pause for effect and watch as the children put down their pencils and look at me with concern. Obviously, I do not use this approach with them very often. This is what helps to guarantee that when I do speak this way, they will listen.

"What I am about to say is never to be repeated to anyone, especially not to the person about whom I am going to speak. This is a private conversation. I am trusting each and every one of you. Do you understand?"

"Yes, Miss Kathleen," they comply. They know me well enough by now to know that I am very serious.

Taking a deep breath, I say, "We need to talk about Cadden. It is why I had him leave the room, but he does not know that and he is not to be told. If ever he comes back before we are finished, we must stop immediately and go back to what we were doing as if nothing happened and we will finish this talk another time. Sometimes it can be seen as rude to talk about someone when they are not around but, in this situation, we are talking about him without him here so that we can help him." My eyes work the room, connecting with each student to be sure that my message is clear. Then I ask, "Clearly, Cadden is hurting. I see how the class tends to leave Cadden out of group work and I have been hearing that Cadden is being picked on in the schoolyard at recess. I know some of you in this class have trouble with him sometimes and I also know that there are kids from other classes who are teasing him.

How many of you have noticed that Cadden is having a tough time fitting in?" This usually prompts a few kids to call out things such as, "I always try to be nice to him, but he says weird things," or "Yeah, but the last time I asked him to be my math partner, he kept showing off that he was faster than me."

"I hear you and I understand your perspective. You are not wrong to feel the way you feel but I would like to teach you something about Cadden that can help you to feel differently about him. Cadden is not always easy to get along with. But let me ask you this, how many of you think it is easy to be Cadden?" I pause briefly, and then I continue, "Have you ever wondered why Cadden says unusual things? What if I told you he doesn't realize what he is doing and that he needs our help and our understanding? Can you imagine not being able to stop yourself from saying things that make people look at you funny? We all say things sometimes that other people don't understand, right? Except, we usually realize that we were misunderstood and we learn from it. But it's not the same for Cadden. He doesn't understand why he isn't understood and he isn't getting enough guidance and support for him to learn otherwise. Imagine for a minute that *to him,* whatever he says and does, makes perfect sense. When he shares his idea out loud, he believes that others are going to laugh with him. But instead, they laugh at him... and then they walk away and ignore him. Or worse, they make fun of him. They say, 'Did you hear what he just said?!' Worse still, they aren't even careful to make sure that he doesn't overhear them laughing at him. How would you feel if you were him?"

There is always someone who will reflect upon this and say, "I wouldn't feel very happy. I'd probably be sad a lot of the time."

Then someone else will say, "Yeah, but why doesn't he just learn to think before he speaks?", to which I will reply, "I am so glad you said that. This is why we are talking about Cadden right now. Your comment is a perfect example of what I mean. It's hard to understand that Cadden does not see the world the way most of us do. We all see things differently, but for Cadden, it's even more different than most of us can imagine. And even if he tries to see it your way, he can't. Can you imagine wanting to be part of the group, but no matter how hard you try, you just get rejected for being too different? If you have never had any trouble making friends and keeping them, then consider yourself lucky. Cadden has been in school for years now, and he still doesn't have one person he can call a good friend."

I let that sink in for a minute. I know there may be another child or two listening to me speak who can actually relate quite well to Cadden's reality. I keep an eye open for those sad faces because I know there will be more work ahead as I address their needs one-on-one in the following days. Cadden is not completely alone in his loneliness. But right now, he is my priority.

Typically, a student will then offer a compassionate comment, such as, "I always help Cadden to find his shoes in the morning," or "Yesterday we let him sit with us at lunch."

I acknowledge these kind gestures and then I get to the point, "I am glad to hear you both saying that. Every little act of kindness matters. I am not asking or telling any of you that you need to be his best friend. Friendship is something that grows naturally and it can't be forced. But being kind to Cadden is something that everyone is capable of and I expect it from each of you."

This is when someone is bound to resist. A student will say something like, "How am I supposed to be nice to him when just yesterday he was telling me he's better than me at math! He was showing off!"

"That is a perfect example of how you can show kindness to Cadden," I reply. "Please try to imagine that Cadden does not know any better. Instead of feeling offended by his words, remind yourself that he's not trying to hurt your feelings. Understand that he has trouble saying things the way that we've learned to say them. What he's probably actually trying to say is, 'Look, here's something I'm good at!' How often does anyone ever pay him a compliment? We might notice that the more kind things we start saying to him, the less he'll feel the need to make those types of comments. What I want everyone to do the next time Cadden says something that sounds like an insult is to help him learn how to say things differently. For example, you could say, 'Cadden, I'd prefer you not say that you are better than me at math, because that kinda hurts my feelings. But, wow, you sure did really well on your math test! Good for you!' Basically, you correct him nicely and then you give him a compliment. How many of you think you can try this?"

Most of the students raise their hands right away. Children have a natural desire to please and to do the right thing. I wrap up our conversation by saying, "I am very confident that I am going to witness a positive change in how Cadden is being treated in class. You'll remember that I said from day one, 'We have an obligation to take care of each other.' What I am most worried about is how he is being treated on the playground. Who is looking out for him? I need to know that you are all taking care of each other on the playground. I am counting on all of you to stand up for him and to advocate for him. I also want you to tell me if someone is bothering him so that I can talk to that child and to his teacher.

"Cadden will be back any minute now. The first and kindest thing you will do for him is to keep this conversation a secret. This is a gift we are giving him." In the weeks ahead, I pay attention to notice the kids who go out of their way for Cadden and I let them know that I see their generosity of spirit and that it is beautiful to witness. I also ask them to notice how it makes them feel. This reinforces the positive behavior.

There is always the possibility that a student may say something to Cadden about our talk, but it's a risk worth taking. If ever Cadden does find out, all I need to do is tell him that we spoke about him because we love him. Nonetheless, I try to nip this problem in the bud by identifying the students I think are at risk for saying something about it to Cadden, and I take each one individually to the side for a heart-to-heart. I'll remind him of a time when he needed my help (or suggest that one day he may need my help) and I'll ask him if he would want everyone to know about it. I'll tell him that I believe I can trust him. I'll ask him if I'm right. Like I said, children are soft-wired to empathize. When we invest in them and we tell them that we trust them to do the right thing, they almost always do.

Within a few days, or sometimes a few hours, Cadden will surely do or say something that will be awkward and someone will try implementing the advice I just gave...but Cadden will not receive it properly. That's to be expected. Cadden is not used to this new approach. He needs to be taught how to receive it. I quietly congratulate the student who modelled the right behavior and then I take Cadden quietly to the side and we have a chat of our own. It goes something like this: "Cadden, you had a rough moment this morning, remember? You were feeling frustrated about the way people were treating you. Can you see that Shannon was trying to help you just now?" I elaborate on how what just took place was an act of kindness. I explain to Cadden that I believe he is going to notice that kids are going to be treating him with more kindness from now on and he needs to make himself available for it.

The 'Caddens' of this world come in different shapes and sizes. Some are more intense than others. All of them deserve our love. Now that I have coached the entire class on what kindness towards our Cadden needs to look like, it will be so much easier to support and coach Cadden's social skills here on in. I have more or less eliminated half of the problem. No solution is ever perfect, but this strategy has served me immensely over the years.

*To change ourselves effectively,
we first had to change our perceptions.*

— Stephen R. Covey

⌘

# Part Four

## The Bigger Picture

New beginnings are available to us on an unlimited basis. As our time together draws to an end, let's take a look at how we can apply the core principles of *Teach Kindness First* on a broader scale.

# 29

# Meet the Teacher Night

WE have covered many issues in this book. Where does this leave us? Let's imagine a fresh school year. Here is my curriculum night or "Meet the Teacher" speech that I have been giving for several years now. It illustrates how we can kick off a new year with this new knowledge in hand.

So many teachers dread information night, but I wish they wouldn't. I get it though -- it is not their natural habitat. They are used to expressing themselves with children. Meanwhile, addressing a room full of adults is a whole other ball game. Many teachers are scared of being put on the spot and questioned unreasonably by over-demanding parents. These are valid concerns, especially since many parents do arrive with an agenda and preconceived ideas about their child's new teacher. And why shouldn't they? In general, parents have only a few opportunities to meet with the teacher without requesting a private meeting. They are entrusting their child to the care of a practical stranger for the next ten months, meaning that many parents are often just as nervous as the teacher, if not more so.

I wish we could all embrace a new philosophy. Parents and teachers must stop fearing one another. Everyone needs to ask themselves where all of these strong emotions are coming from in the first place. Are you scared you don't know what you are doing? Are you worried you won't be good enough? Do you fear that you are not cut out for this job? These are all valid questions, and there is a good chance that *parents and teach-*

*ers alike* would all answer a resounding, "Yes!" The truth is that, by and large, we all have similar worries and these worries ought to unite us rather than divide us. If you aren't the least bit aware that you will make mistakes day in and day out, then you need a serious wake-up call. None of us are perfect. *The more I learn, the less I know.* That is one of my mantras.

Teachers and parents alike need to become comfortable in admitting to their weaknesses if they are ever to have a positive and healthy relationship with one another. My goals for this evening reach far beyond explaining the curriculum. My primary focus is to put parents at ease and to establish a culture of empathy and kindness. Here is a glimpse into what I have found works well for me.

## Where Do We Start?

By now you have surely noticed that I am quite fond of motivational quotes. In the first week of school, I prepare a bag full of quotes, each on individual strips of paper. Each student picks a quote from the bag at random and redesigns it in his own way, choosing images which help to illustrate the meaning of the message. (As an aside, though the child is free to switch his quote if he doesn't connect with or understand it, it is amazing to see how perfectly the quotes they choose at random tend to match the child.) As parents enter my classroom, these motivational quotes are on the walls, hanging from the ceiling, and posted to doors and windows. Some kids even have quotes taped to their desks. As the parents settle in, I draw their attention to these personalized posters, letting them know that their children and I use them as reminders to recenter us and ground us in our thinking and our choices.

Obviously I begin by addressing the curriculum and routine practices, but most of that is presented in a slideshow on the Smart Board in the first five minutes. In fact, one of my favorite things to do is to send home information letters which explain quite a bit about the curriculum and "housekeeping" items *prior* to Meet the Teacher Night. This way, I can simply ask parents if they have any questions about the information that has been sent home. Nobody enjoys being read to and nobody is looking for a dry evening of facts and lists. I always have at least one parent who will comment something to the effect of, "I noticed that you aren't using a math workbook. When I was a kid, we always had a workbook."

I'll reply, "Basically, you are pointing to the fact that the way we teach today is quite different from the way we were taught as kids. It takes getting used to, I know. Throughout the year you will surely notice that some of my teaching strategies are somewhat unconventional. I want you to know that my practices are rooted in current educational research, specifically about our understanding of how children learn differently from one another and how the skills they need for the future are quite different from the ones we thought we needed when we were students. It would be irresponsible of me to teach the children of today the way we were taught as kids. Your children are being prepared for a world that none of us can imagine. You will notice that as I introduce new concepts to the students, I will send out an email explaining the theory and purpose of what we are doing, coupled with strategies that your child is being taught to use. I am always happy to answer your questions and concerns, but please be sure to read my emails thoroughly first in order to use our time wisely."

Unless the parents have more questions on the matter, I don't usually spend much more time on curriculum questions. Personally, when I sit in on nights like these as a parent, my number one concern is to make sure that my child is in good hands. Of course I want the teacher to be competent in whatever subjects she is teaching, but I know that none of that will matter if my child does not feel safe and welcomed in her classroom.

One of the first things I tell parents is that I have already fallen in love with their children (and that's the truth). I describe the dynamic of the group in a positive light, no matter what. For instance, even if they are a challenging group, I'll say that they are an energetic bunch. And if by chance the dynamic of the group is above average, I refrain from saying things like, "I haven't had such a strong group of students in years." That can be construed as offensive. Families are often composed of several children. Comparing classes is paramount to comparing their children. That's a major *faux-pas*. I never single out any students. I share no personal information such as how many kids are on individual educational plans or how many are diagnosed with disabilities. That is private information. My mission is to put parents at ease, not on guard. I want them to put their faith in me and I make it clear that I am putting my faith in them. These precious thirty minutes I have with the parents set a tone for the entire year.

## Transparency

I let the parents know that I believe in transparency. "I have nothing to hide...ever," I tell them, "I am human. I humbly admit that I will make mistakes. Moreover, your children will make mistakes....probably daily. So as much as you may like to be kept abreast of everything that goes on in the classroom, I need you to trust my judgment. It would be physically impossible for me to report each perceived infraction that occurs for each child. What's more, you should not want me to. You deserve to enjoy the few hours you have with your child in the evening as much as possible. Every problem of which I make you aware is one that you then need to deal with, and that can be exhausting and challenging, especially since you weren't there to witness it. That is why I do my best to handle problems as they arise. So long as I feel the issue has been resolved and it's of no huge concern, then I believe you really don't need to know about it. In general, a child will get three chances before I will contact a parent. This seems fair and reasonable. Children need to be given a chance to prove themselves. We all deserve a 'free pass' every now and then. So if I call you and I report a series of events that has led up to that phone call, I need you to understand that it is not reasonable to ask me why I didn't call you when the first thing happened. The expression 'hindsight is 20/20' exists for a good reason. We cannot predict that a pattern will emerge until it does. What's more, I need you to know, and trust, that when I call home to talk to you, it is because I am looking for collaboration and support. I am not interested in finger-pointing. I am looking for solutions to help your child overcome whatever challenge he is facing. I am a firm believer in natural consequences. My aim is to motivate your child to want what's best for himself. I am not out to get him. I am his guide, his cheerleader, his supporter; I am not his enemy."

I tell parents, "I am the kind of person who wears her heart on her sleeve. You can tell by the way I am speaking with you tonight just how enthusiastic and emotional I am. With this in mind, I beg of you to think twice before you write me an email that could be interpreted as aggressive or accusatory. If your child comes home telling you a story about something bad that happened and you think to yourself, 'Oh my goodness! How could the teacher have let this happen?' or 'Why wasn't I told?' I beg of you to hold on a minute before you jump the gun. I often check my email before the kids arrive, so if I am greeted with a rude or accusatory email, I promise you that my ability to teach effectively will be compromised. You do not want that for the kids. Just as I will always give you and your child the benefit of the doubt, I ask you do to the same for me. If you have a concern, by all means write or call me, but do so kindly and politely, just as I would towards you. For example, instead of saying, 'How come you didn't tell me that my daughter was pushed to the ground at recess today?' you could write, 'Jessica told me she was pushed in the schoolyard at recess and she was quite hurt. Did she tell you about this? Is there anything else you can tell me about it? Thank you for your time.'

"We've all been kids before and we've all changed the details of a story to help make sure we don't get in trouble. No parent ever really wants to be told that their child isn't telling the truth, but the truth is that children will tell their story from their perspective and it will be true to them. I always say, 'Every event has at least three versions - mine, yours and the truth!' By communicating with me politely, by asking questions and avoiding jumping to conclusions, I get to respond as efficiently and effectively as possible without wasting energy on feeling offended or attacked, and I don't need to waste precious teaching time on long-winded explanations.

"Over the years I have come to realize that the tone of an email can be especially difficult to interpret when you do not know the person very well. So if ever you get a message from me and you think I have written it aggressively or with a 'tone', I am promising you right now, that was unintentional. Perhaps I wrote it too quickly and did not reread it enough to realize how it could be misinterpreted. I promise to always be professional with you and I will never intentionally have a negative attitude. So just as I ask you to give me the benefit of the doubt, I, too, will accord you the same courtesy."

There is always at least one parent in the group who is skilled at keeping the mood light and will make a joke along the lines of, "Don't worry, my child never tells me anything about his day anyways! Hahaha!" We all laugh, as most of us can relate to this statement. Then, being the teacher that I am, I'll reply,

"I've experienced that with my kids, too. You would think that if you ask them about their day immediately after school that there ought to be something they could tell us about it. Yet, how often do we just get a shoulder shrug or a simple, 'Fine.'" More laughter ensues.

"What I've found, though, is that later on, when we sit down to dinner all together, that's when the highlights of the day get shared. I don't know if you know this, but studies have shown that the family meal is a clear indicator of school success. It's something to keep in mind. I have also noticed that my kids tend to be most comfortable talking about their problems at night. It seems like that's when they are taking stock of their day, and a heart-to-heart at bedtime is when they are finally ready to deal with it. I guess what I'm saying is that the more opportunities we create for our kids to talk to us, the more likely it is that they will. We just have to keep at it and make ourselves available as often as possible."

I let parents know that I'm hoping to be a source of support to them. I want them to see that I can relate to the realities of raising children. I recognize that teaching and parenting have their own specific challenges. I try to keep in mind that while I may have taught over a hundred 8-year-olds, this may be the first 8-year-old for whom they have ever been responsible.

## Consequences

Parents often ask me about what kind of consequences they can expect. For instance, they want to know if I keep kids in at recess. My reply is as follows, "I believe in natural consequences. Natural consequences can mean that when the children are cooperating and doing their best, there's likely to be time for extra fun activities at the end of the day. But a natural consequence can also mean the loss of a privilege. It breaks my heart to see a child miss recess, especially since I am a firm believer in the need to move and get fresh air to rejuvenate ourselves and be ready for more learning; and I tell the children as much. However, if a student decides to use his work time to play, then he, in turn, will be expected to use his play time to work. If that means he misses recess, well, that is the choice he made for himself. I believe children must take responsibility for their choices. In fact, at times, when I deem it necessary, your child will be required to email you about his behavior and it will require an acknowledgment of receipt from you. This way, we completely avoid the whole 'he-said, she-said' which can occur when a teacher reports a problem. Rather, your child may email you saying, 'I was fooling around in class when I should have been working so I needed to finish my work at recess. Next time, I will be more responsible about getting my work done.' I have found that parents really appreciate this kind of communication since it makes it harder for the child to make excuses for his behavior. Sometimes I will have your child dictate his words to me and I will type for him, to speed up the process. By emailing you directly, it avoids chasing papers and it ensures that you get prompt notification of an important issue.

"That reminds me, you may have noticed that I do not work with a point system. I want children to do the right thing - tidy their desk, finish their work, or whatever the case may be - because it is the right thing to do, not because it's going to get them some kind of prize from the dollar store. I want us all to be our best because that's how it should be, not because some chart says we should be. Plus, the charts tend to work mostly for the kids who are already good at doing these things. Those who find personal management difficult only become more frustrated and often regress when they see their peers consistently earning more points than them. In my opinion, point charts completely disregard the fact that fair does not mean equal. Each child will have his own personal goals that he and I will choose together at the beginning of the term, and he will be reminded of these goals throughout the term. I have seen real growth take place since I implemented this strategy, so I know it works.

"Basically, it all ties into making your child feel secure and safe in the classroom. He ought to feel respected and honored, and a big part of that comes from not being compared to others. Rather, the only person he should ever compare himself to is himself. This is why I incorporate dancing, singing, yoga, meditation, and mindfulness into our daily routine. We all live lives outside of these four walls and it isn't always easy to separate the two, yet it can be a very healthy practice. I want your children to know that they are safe to relax and take chances in this classroom. I do not tolerate teasing. We celebrate mistakes. A mistake means that you took a chance and tried. The underlying message is always the same in that we show kindness towards ourselves by trying our best and we show kindness towards others by allowing them to take chances without fear of being ridiculed."

I have said a lot, I know, and yet I have still not said all that I would like to say. Now that I have a blog and a book, I invite parents to consult them for additional insights into my philosophies and practices.

On that note, let's stop calling curriculum night by its less than flattering title "Meet the Creature Night". I have a great sense of humor, but this play on words is just so sad to me. If that is sincerely how everyone feels about it then we are all in big trouble. If you leave your child's classroom feeling that this catchphrase is appropriate, then I advise you to speak to the principal about your concerns. And teachers, if you leave your classroom feeling like a creature, then I advise you to rethink your approach.

*Kind words can be short and easy to speak, but their echoes are truly endless.*

– Mother Teresa

⌘

# 30

# When We Know Better

I have touched upon the issue of bullying a few times throughout this book because it is a very real problem that demands a fresh approach. Bullying is not going to go away - it *cannot* go away - until a shared philosophy of teaching kindness first is put in place in all of our education centers. By now, I think I've made it clear that the solution to finding more peace in our homes and schools starts with how adults communicate, not just with children, but with each other as well. At the root of how we communicate with each other are our belief systems. We must question our beliefs and adapt ourselves accordingly if we are to experience a true, positive change in how we treat one another. In order to clarify and attest to this point, I will share the story of when I was bullied.

When I was in the eighth grade and a trio of ninth-grade girls began harassing me, I did not know what to do. I tried to ignore it, but that did nothing to appease them. At first, it just felt like teasing. However, the less I reacted to them, the worse the taunting became. They would push me in the hall, make me drop my books, and call me names. I would come to learn that my recent friendship with Ethan, the new boy in school, was perceived as a threat to Natasha, one of these three girls who, unbeknownst to me, had a huge crush on him. My Home Economics class was a blended group of grade eight and nine students. We were seated in alphabetical order, which meant that Ethan and I were seated side-by-side at the front of the class while Natasha was seated in the far back corner. Ethan had a wicked sense of humor, and in those few minutes before class would get started, Ethan and I would chat. I guess Natasha didn't appreciate the way I laughed at his jokes. Her jealousy prompted her to enlist a couple of her friends to intimidate me, in the hopes that I would stop talking to him. Needless to say, that was a futile endeavour. Once I understood why this anger was being sent my way, what was I supposed to do? Was I supposed to say, "Ethan, please stop being my friend so that Natasha and her little gang will stop bullying me?" Maybe that *is* something I should have tried, but Natasha had picked her target well. I was a quiet girl who kept out of trouble and who avoided conflict at all costs. It's not as if I was the only other girl with whom Ethan spoke. Natasha clearly had bigger issues with which she was struggling, and she had found a perfect outlet for her frustrations.

As the weeks went by, the taunting continued to escalate until, one morning, I arrived at school to find cruel words scrawled across my locker. That was when a couple of my close friends insisted I take action. "Stop letting them treat you like this, Kathy. You need to stand up to them." That day, I made a new discovery. I realized that I was being kinder to them than I was being to myself. As we took in the sight of the slurs scrawled on my locker, the looks on my friends' faces pushed me to love myself better. I could see the sadness of the situation reflected in their eyes. It was as if the veil had been lifted and I finally understood that I was playing the role of the perfect victim. Later that day, one of Natasha's allies, Brittany, approached me with a rolled up magazine in hand. Hitting the magazine loudly into her opposite hand, she threatened, "I should just slap you across the face with this!" All I could do was stare at her, dumbfounded. I (finally) knew that I didn't deserve this. As I turned my back to her and headed off early to my next class, I made up my mind. I needed this to end. I secretly wished that she would just go ahead and hit me. It was just myself and a good friend of mine who were sitting in the otherwise empty classroom when Brittany and Samantha, the third girl in the trio, came in looking for me. She walked right up to me and followed through on her threat. I snapped. I hit back. Me.

Hitting someone. Me. The kid who felt guilty killing a mosquito. I can still hear the sound of Mr. Preston's voice as he entered the room and took in the scene before him. "Kathy Murray??? What's going on here? Stop it, girls! You need to stop! You all need to go to the office. Right now!" The disbelief in his voice at seeing me engaged in a physical fight spoke well to the situation. It was indeed surreal.

The principal required all of us to write out our version of the events. Once she had read through each of our accounts, she gave us all a detention. I could not believe it! I had never, ever, had a detention for anything. What was I in trouble for exactly? For defending myself? The principal explained to me that these girls would only keep bothering me if they were to see that I got off scot-free. I saw her point but it still seemed terribly unfair. I was already a victim. Of course, I can't know what other measures may have taken place, such as phone calls or meetings with the parents of these girls, but the bullying came to an end. However, there's a surprising and unexpected twist to this story. A couple of years later, we would all find ourselves on a bus headed off to "Leadership Camp".

## The Apology

I still recall my shock at realizing that these girls were on this trip as well. I remember thinking to myself, "How is it possible that they are being offered leadership roles? They are so mean!" My first evening at camp was spent avoiding them as much as possible, and I can't even explain my sense of relief when I saw that, thankfully, we would not be sharing the same dormitory. The next morning, as I headed towards the mess hall for breakfast, there was Natasha, heading straight towards me with two steaming cups in hand. "Do you drink coffee?" she called out to me. I cannot remember making any kind of intelligent answer. I was too stunned to speak. "I took a chance and added one milk, one sugar," she continued, handing me the cup. I don't put sugar in my coffee, but I told her that's exactly how I liked it, and I sipped it gratefully. "I know it's strange for all of us to be here together," she said, handing me the cup. "Look, I need to apologize to you. It was really stupid the way we treated you. I was dealing with some crappy stuff at home and I took it out on you. That wasn't cool of me. I'm really sorry and so are Brittany and Samantha. They'll talk to you later, but I really wanted to talk to you first since it was all my fault to begin with."

I still get a lump in my throat when I tell this story. It was such a beautiful moment. Not everyone gets to have an apology from their victimizer. That, in itself, was a gift and allowed me to have closure on that unpleasant chapter in my life. As I watched Natasha walk towards me that day at camp, my feet felt the urge to run away, but something inside of me forced me to stay. Instead of giving in to the feeling of fear, I paid attention to my gut that whispered, "Give her a chance." In so doing, I allowed for a powerful transformation to take place, not only for myself, but for Natasha and the other girls as well.

## I Should Have Asked for Help

You may be wondering why I didn't just ask for help from a teacher. I think it had a lot to do with the culture of the school. I'm not implying anything negative against my school. I'm proud of my high school and I had some fabulous teachers. It was just a different era. Personally, I have zero recollection of teachers talking to us about what to do if we felt we were being bullied. I know for certain that teachers were in the hallways when these girls were calling out mean things and pushing me around. Not one teacher intervened. The belief system in place back then, as I understand it, was that some kids are going to be mean. It was just normal.

It also had to do with how I was being raised. Although I felt close to my dad, this didn't feel like the kind of thing I would talk to him about. In my mind, some of the names they were calling me were far too embarrassing to repeat, especially to a man. Meanwhile, my mom and I had a strained relationship. Prior to this situation, I remember trying to talk to my mom about my life. Somehow, she would find a way to turn things around and make it seem like I was doing something wrong.

Being bullied by these girls was one of the worst things that had happened to me so far. Even if it was only on an unconscious level, I figured I was somehow to blame. Ultimately, in my mind, I had no reason to believe that anyone could help me. (Parents, please heed my warning. By being too demanding, too strict, or too rigid, you risk cutting yourself off from your child. The very thing you fear the most is that much more likely to materialize because you weren't available to catch the warning signs and actually be there for your child when she needed you the most. I was lucky. My story ends well.)

## When We Know Better, We Do Better

I have no regrets as to how this situation played itself out. I learned several valuable lessons which have shaped who I am today. I am sure the same goes for Natasha, Brittany, and Samantha. But the turn of events begs the question: where did the motivation to apologize to me come from for these girls? Better yet, *who* was the driving force behind their apologies?

I don't pretend to know all the factors that prepared them to ask for my forgiveness, but I do know that Mr. Drummond, the main organizer of the leadership camp, played an important role in it. Mr. Drummond was a teacher who spoke kindly and treated students fairly, but he was no pushover. Brave was the soul who would choose to challenge him on any issue of social justice. He had zero tolerance for lack of kindness in his classroom. He had a knack for identifying the students who were in need of help and he would inspire them to get involved in leadership activities. He understood that if you wanted to motivate students to make better choices, then you should put them in a leadership role. He gave Natasha and her friends a sense of purpose which allowed them to see that being helpful around school was more rewarding and satisfying than getting into trouble and causing pain to others.

This begs an even bigger question: why was Mr. Drummond one of the few teachers helping children to channel their energy in positive, constructive ways? Why was this not a shared goal for every adult in the building? It is time we all agree that the primary mission of being involved in the lives of children is to ensure that we are guiding and supporting them to be the best, *kindest* people they can be.

## It Begins with Us

At the beginning of this chapter I said that change needs to start with the adults. Because our children are watching us. We are their models. They are our mirrors. Therefore, to talk about bullying by first considering the role of the paid professional seems like a fair and reasonable thing to do. If we truly wish to teach our children how to advocate for themselves, then they need to feel safe doing so. When everyone agrees that we must treat each other with kindness, the culture of the school will change in a dramatic way. It is not enough to just say we believe in being kind. We must agree to hold ourselves and each other accountable.

If a shared philosophy about the energy and the attitudes accepted in my high school had existed and been embraced by the entire staff, my experience with those girls would have certainly been very different. When *all* the students know that *all* the adults will enforce a policy of kindness, it affects the actions and reactions of everyone in the building. That's not to say no one will ever make a mistake and be unkind. But the chain of events following an unkind act would unfold in a much more loving way. It would not have mattered which adult had witnessed the first sign of aggression. In a culture of kindness first, anyone who witnesses a conflict learns to feel comfortable speaking up. It could be any adult or any student who may simply ask if we are all okay or if we need any help. A gentle expression of concern would have reminded all four of us that we are never alone in our suffering and a support system is always available.

Even the caretakers ought to be trained in empathy and kindness. Who do you think cleaned the mean words off my locker? Our caretakers often see what teachers do not. They see the stragglers in the hallways and in the washrooms, while teachers are in their classrooms teaching. Most problems occur when kids think nobody *who cares* is watching. Imagine how different things would have been if the caretaker (or any other adult in the school) had greeted me at my locker and taken charge of the situation. How was it possible that not even one adult came to ask me about what was going on *before* I was pushed to my breaking point?

It is time to make teaching through kindness and empathy an integral and obligatory aspect of any program that involves working with and around children. Until adults are taught and obliged to treat children with greater respect and kindness, we have no good reason to expect a decrease in bullying. As it stands right now, in any given school, there are conflicting ideas and philosophies about bullying. Positive, measurable change will only occur when every single adult in a childcare or educational facility agrees that the starting point for change lies in unifying how we talk to the students, and that the core of this belief lies in practicing kindness, first and foremost. If even just one adult in a facility is perceived by the students as mean, rude or, worse, a bully, how can the situation for the kids ever hope to improve?

It's time we start using the same toolbox. We need to build positive relationships with children. *Children do not come into our lives to make our lives easy.* We are all here to help each other grow. If we want kids to keep improving themselves, then we must improve ourselves and the way we communicate. It starts with us choosing a unified path of kindness.

*The secret of change is to focus all of your energy,*
*not on fighting the old,*
*but on building the new.*

– Dan Millman

⌘

# 31

# Where Do We Start?

I recently heard the story of an African community where, rather than punishing someone for their mistakes, its citizens assemble in the heart of the village, surround the sinner while chanting spiritual songs, and remind the sinner of their innate goodness. Their belief is that it is not the will of the sinner to have sinned. The sin is a symptom of detachment from the spiritual world. They come together as a people to heal one another. What a beautiful practice. Instead of focusing on punitive measures, they guide the sinner to reconnect with his heart and soul.

Imagine if children were to learn at a young age to not take anything personally so that when a child got pushed, hit, or called a name, he would respond by saying, "Whoa, what's wrong? Can I help? Want to talk about it?" It is a simple, kind, and loving response. It serves to put out a fire before it ever begins. We give children an amazing gift when we teach them to be loving to themselves. When pain is sent our way, we do not have to accept it. We can choose to stay connected to our heart. When we choose love over pain, it can then feel natural to reach out to our offender. Kindness helps us to protect ourselves and simultaneously helps heal those around us.

As humans, we share the common bond of being imperfect. We also share the common bond of wanting to be seen and to be understood. The better we get at accepting ourselves, the better we get at accepting others. It goes hand in hand. The next time someone upsets you, rather than joining them in their pain, ask yourself what is hurting them and why should their words have the power to hurt you? Empathy is the gateway to being kind. Kindness is the gateway to having more joy and love in your heart.

## Let's Begin

In my introduction, I claimed that 1 - There is a knowingness that something is missing from our society, 2 - That everything happens for a reason and we must embrace the lesson, and 3 - That happiness is a choice. The stories and conversations I shared with you served to illustrate these axioms, but we do not need to wait for a problem to arise in order to begin practicing kindness in our daily lives. Allow me to offer three simple guidelines we can follow in our daily lives to attract kindness and be happier.

## 1 - Be the Light

There is a knowingness that something is missing from our society. By now, I hope we all agree that kindness is the source for bringing greater joy and happiness to our lives. One of the simplest ways to bring more kindness into our lives is to create it ourselves, so my first challenge to you is to set yourself the goal of brightening someone's day, each and every day, through random acts of kindness. This commitment is almost guaranteed to have a positive impact on your daily life, as well as those who receive the kindness, and everyone who witnesses it. And if you would like to take this even further, why not create interactive, visual reminders to celebrate the kindness you give and receive? In a home, you could have a chalkboard in the kitchen where you and your family write loving messages and inspiring quotes for each other. In a school, there could be bulletin boards entitled "Kindness is..." and "Today I..." where everyone is invited to record acts of kindness, as well as messages of hope and forgiveness. Throughout the building there could be posters which read, "Be loving!", "Joy is contagious, spread it around!", "Smiles are free, pay it forward!", "All you need is love!" and "It's cool to care!" Focussing our attention on who we want to be and how we want to feel, and then acting upon it, is surely the single best course of action we can take to bring more joy and happiness back into society.

## 2 - No More Excuses

The second goal I identified was embracing the lessons life offers us. We can choose to learn these lessons, or we can can choose to resist them. I say, let's choose to learn the lessons and live life to the fullest. In so doing, we help prevent, or at least minimize, future conflicts. Part of learning the lesson is accepting responsibility for the role we played. So the second challenge I am offering you is to learn how to apologize authentically when the situation merits it (and since it takes two to tango, most situations do.) Make the commitment that every time you find yourself engaging negatively in a conflict, you will look within yourself to question your negative reaction. This will allow you to own your behavior and apologize authentically. No one is immune from moments of over-indulging their Ego and ignoring their True Self. Fear is often at the root of anger and frustration. Love allows us to be forgiving, not only of ourselves, but of others as well. To be authentic means that we must avoid making an excuse within our apology. Pay attention to when your apology uses words such as "but", "except", "however", and so on, and rephrase your apology accordingly. The better we get at apologizing authentically, the better we become at owning our role in any situation. The act of identifying our role sends the message to ourselves and others that we are growing in our awareness. In so doing, we set up better conditions for avoiding a similar problem in the future. I'm not saying that this is the be-all and end-all of conflicts. But it's a good start in prevention. Consider the following apologies.

"I'm sorry I screamed at you but you made me so angry."

"I hope you can forgive me for losing my patience but you just wouldn't listen."

"I feel terrible about what I said to you earlier but when you use that tone of voice with me I just can't take it."

Let's pause for a moment to consider how the recipient of these apologies could feel. I doubt they feel like a true resolution has taken place. Without resolution, even if we are agreeing to move on from this problem, we've only really just swept it under the rug. It will likely resurface again and play itself out in a similar pattern. However, if we break the pattern and own our role in the conflict, we grow from it, and growth is progress. Being authentic doesn't have to be complicated either. Consider these reformulations of the previous apologies:

"I'm sorry I screamed at you."

"I hope you can forgive me for losing my patience."

"I feel terrible about what I said to you earlier."

Don't these apologies feel lighter and more genuine? There's an absence of excuses, and therefore an absence of blame. There's just an honest acknowledgment of one's own behavior. I think this is a good start. It is kind, and it paves the way for progressively kinder and more peaceful resolutions in the future.

**Our prime purpose in this life is to help others. And if you can't help them, at least don't hurt them.**

– Dalai Lama

## 3 - Laugh Whenever Possible

My third and last proposed idea is that happiness is a choice. What better way to feel happier than to laugh as often as possible in a day? Laughter is food for the soul. It's especially helpful to learn to laugh at ourselves when we make a mistake. There is nothing quite so liberating and uplifting as a heartfelt laugh. Sharing a laugh with someone brings us closer to them. It builds positive relationships and keeps us healthy. The better we get at finding humor in a situation, the more joyful we will likely feel. The more joyful we feel, the more acts of kindness we are likely to perform. The more acts of kindness we perform, the more likely others around us will be inspired to do the same. It's an upward spiral motion of goodness.

**There is nothing in the world so irresistibly contagious as laughter and good humor.**

– Charles Dickens

## There Is So Much More to Say

The raising and teaching of children is our most important task. Every day comes with new challenges. Difficult conversations are a guarantee, but hopefully we now have the tools to help us navigate them with greater ease and confidence. We will not see eye to eye on everything. From opinions on how much homework is too much, to missing school for vacations or sporting events, we all have, and will continue to have, varying opinions on what is best. It's how we go about discussing these issues that makes the difference between living together harmoniously or feeling like we are constantly fighting an uphill battle. We need to expect to disagree with each other on a regular basis - that's what allows us to challenge ourselves and grow.

'Cause our children are watching us
They put their trust in us
They're gonna be like us
So let's learn from our history
And do it differently.

– Dixie Chicks

⌘

# Final Words, For Now

I promised I would only speak of what I know to be true, and that is what I have done. If even just one of these stories has inspired you to be kinder to yourself and to others, and to go through your day in a more gentle and loving way, then I'm one step closer to my goal of living in a kinder world. I hope I have convinced you that how we communicate with one another matters. I never said it was easy. I'm still learning, too. It's an art. Like anything, it takes practice to get better. I am convinced that it is one of the best ways to live a happier life. Everybody deserves kindness. Everybody is worthy of love. And those who challenge this belief the most are the ones who need it the most.

We must never underestimate the power we have in turning a child's life around. We may expect them to "know better" but here's what I say to that: No matter what we feel they ought to know, in any given situation, we should still know *more*. By default, we will always have more life experience than a child, so we always owe it to them to take the time to listen to their story and to prove that we care about their success. They will fall down. We must pick them up. We must prove to them how much we care. Over and over again. Before we can expect more kindness and empathy from children, we must expect more of ourselves. When we take the time to engage children in problem-solving through kindness and empathy, we empower them with skills that will serve them for a lifetime. I love imagining these kinder and more empathetic children as the leaders of tomorrow. I can't wait to live in that world!

I trust that this book illustrates how to implement the core principles of communicating kindly in a concrete fashion. My daughters are growing older and as they do, a wealth of stories await. I invite you to follow me on my blog at teachkindnessfirst.com as we continue on this journey. Send me your questions and share with me your success stories as life throws you new challenges.

If you retain only one idea from this book, I hope that it is this: kindness begins with you. Never mistake kindness for weakness. It can take far more strength to hold back angry thoughts than to just speak our mind. To be human is to err. All I ask is that when we do lose our patience, that we be willing to own our behavior. We are responsible for the energy we bring into any environment, be it our homes, our schools, or our community. Make "be kind" the mantra of your life. The reality is that everyone is just doing their best, including you. With kindness as our guide, this thing called life promises to get better and better.

> *One is loved because one is loved.*
> *No reason is needed for loving.*
>
> – Paulo Coelho

⌘

## References and Recommended Reading

*"A Cherokee Legend - Two Wolves."* Pinterest, www.pinterest.com/pin/174514554284390310/.

BrainyQuote. *BrainyQuote,* 2001-2016, http://www.brainyquote.com/quotes/favorites.html.

Brown, Brené. *The Gifts of Imperfection.* Hazelden, 2010.

Brown, Brené. *"The power of vulnerability".* TED, June 2010, www.ted.com/talks/brene_brown_on_vulnerability?language=en.

Chicks, Dixie. "I Hope." *Taking the Long Way,* Sony Music Nashville, 2006.

Cole, Nat King. "Nature Boy." *Best of Nat King Cole,* Capitol Records, 1947.

Covey, Stephen M. R., and Rebecca R. Merrill. *The Speed of Trust: The One Thing That Changes Everything.* Free Press, 2008. www.goodreads.com/quotes/147819-we-judge-ourselves-by-our-intentions-and-others-by-their

Kipp, Mastin. *"Love is Not the Opposite of Fear!"* Mastin Kipp's Daily Love, 27 Nov. 2013, thedailylove.com/love-is-not-the-opposite-of-fear/.

Kottler, Jeffrey A. *The Language of Tears.* Jossey-Bass Publishers, 1996.

Kurcinka, Mary Sheedy. *Raising Your Spirited Child: A Guide for Parents Whose Child Is More Intense, Sensitive, Perceptive, Persistent, Energetic.* Harper, 2006.

Kurcinka, Mary Sheedy. *Sleepless in America: Is Your Child Misbehaving or Missing Sleep?* HarperCollins, 2006.

Lifevestinside. *"Life Vest Inside - Kindness Boomerang - 'One Day' "*. YouTube, 29 Aug. 2011, www.youtube.com/watch?v=nwAYpLVyeFU.

Morrish, Ronald G. *With All Due Respect: Keys for Building Effective School Discipline.* Woodstream Pub., 2000.

*Online thesaurus.* Dictionary.com, 2016, www.dictionary.com/browse/online-thesaurus.

Quote Investigator. *Quote Investigator: Exploring The Origins of Quotes.* http://quoteinvestigator.com/.

*Random Acts of Kindness.* The Random Acts of Kindness Foundation, 2016, www.randomactsofkindness.org/.

Rifkin, Jeremy. *"The empathic civilization."* TED, Aug. 2010, www.ted.com/talks/jeremy_rifkin_on_the_empathic_civilization.

Robinson, Ken. *Out of Our Minds: Learning to Be Creative.* Capstone, 2011.

Ruiz, Miguel. *The Four Agreements: A Practical Guide to Personal Freedom.* Amber-Allen Pub., 1997.

Sinek, Simon. *"How great leaders inspire action."* TED, Sept. 2009, www.ted.com/talks/simon_sinek_how_great_leaders_inspire_action.

Taylor, Clem, Ann Varney, Art Rubalcava, and Eric M. Strauss, writers. *What Would You Do?* ABC, 2008.

Tolle, Eckhart. *A New Earth: Awakening to Your Life's Purpose.* Thorndike Press, 2005.

Tsabary, Shefali. *The Conscious Parent: Transforming Ourselves, Empowering Our Children.* Namaste Pub., 2010.

Whitaker, Todd. *What Great Teachers Do Differently: 14 Things That Matter Most.* Eye on Education, 2004.

Winget, Larry. *Shut Up, Stop Whining & Get a Life. A Kick-Butt Approach to a Better Life.* John Wiley & Sons, Inc., 2011.

Winget, Larry. *Your Kids Are Your Own Fault: a Fix-the-Way-You-Parent Guide for Raising Responsible, Productive Adults.* Gotham Books, 2010.

*"Your 6-month-old's development."* BabyCenter, 1997-2016, www.babycenter. ca/a721/your-6-month-olds-development.

NOTE ON SOURCES: Every reasonable effort has been given to accredit each quote to its original author. However, a variety of versions of similar sayings or expressions arise over the centuries, making it challenging at times to be certain of who said what first. When in doubt, diligent effort has been made to go as far back in time as possible in order to find the most original form of the saying. In certain cases, an expression is so common, and has been around for so long, that no specific author can be identified. In these cases, the quotes have been attributed to Popular Wisdom. Moreover, Quotes Investigator, goodreads and BrainyQuote were the most common reference tools used in cases where the quote derived from a particular author were found online without knowing or having consulted the original source (i.e. from which book the quote was taken).

# About the Author

Kathleen Murray was born and raised in the suburbs of Montreal, Canada. After getting her B.Ed. from McGill University, she travelled across Canada, teaching in Toronto and Vancouver. She has since settled in Quebec and is currently a third-grade teacher of the International Baccalaureate program at Children's World Academy in Lasalle. She has more than 15 years of experience in the classroom and she has been passionate about teaching for as long as she can remember.

Her greatest joy comes from witnessing random acts of kindness, be it from children or adults.

She lives in Chateauguay with her amazingly supportive husband and their two lovely daughters.